PENGUIN ENTERPRISE

THREAD BY THREAD

Thread By Thread is a personal look into the journey of Shambhu Kumar, who, starting from scratch built one of India's most successful textile empires. The book traces his growth from being a trader to an industrialist checking the milestones on the way to reveal the business mantra that lies behind his phenomenal success. A tribute to S.Kumars' founder in its 75th year, the book is based on interviews with family, friends, colleagues and employees.

THREAD BY THREAD

The S.Kumars Story

SATHYA SARAN

PENGUIN
ENTERPRISE

An imprint of Penguin Random House

PENGUIN ENTERPRISE

USA | Canada | UK | Ireland | Australia
New Zealand | India | South Africa | China | Singapore

Penguin Enterprise is part of the Penguin Random House group of companies
whose addresses can be found at global.penguinrandomhouse.com

Published by Penguin Random House India Pvt. Ltd
4th Floor, Capital Tower 1, MG Road,
Gurugram 122 002, Haryana, India

Penguin
Random House
India

First published in Penguin Enterprise by Penguin Random House India 2023

Project Head: Vidhi Kasliwal
Writer & Editor: Sathya Saran
Editorial Assistants: Devroop Sharma, Nilesh Bhatkar

Cover Image: Manoj Jain
Back Cover Image: Saaket Dhongade

10 9 8 7 6 5 4 3 2 1

The views and opinions expressed in this book are the author's own and the
facts are as reported by her which have been verified to the extent possible,
and the publishers are not in any way liable for the same.

ISBN 9780143464433

Design & Layout by Mary Varghees
Printed at Thomson Press India Ltd, New Delhi

www.penguin.co.in

DEDICATED TO ALL THE TEAM
MEMBERS OF S.KUMARS WHO
HAVE CONTRIBUTED TO ITS
75 YEARS OF SUCCESS

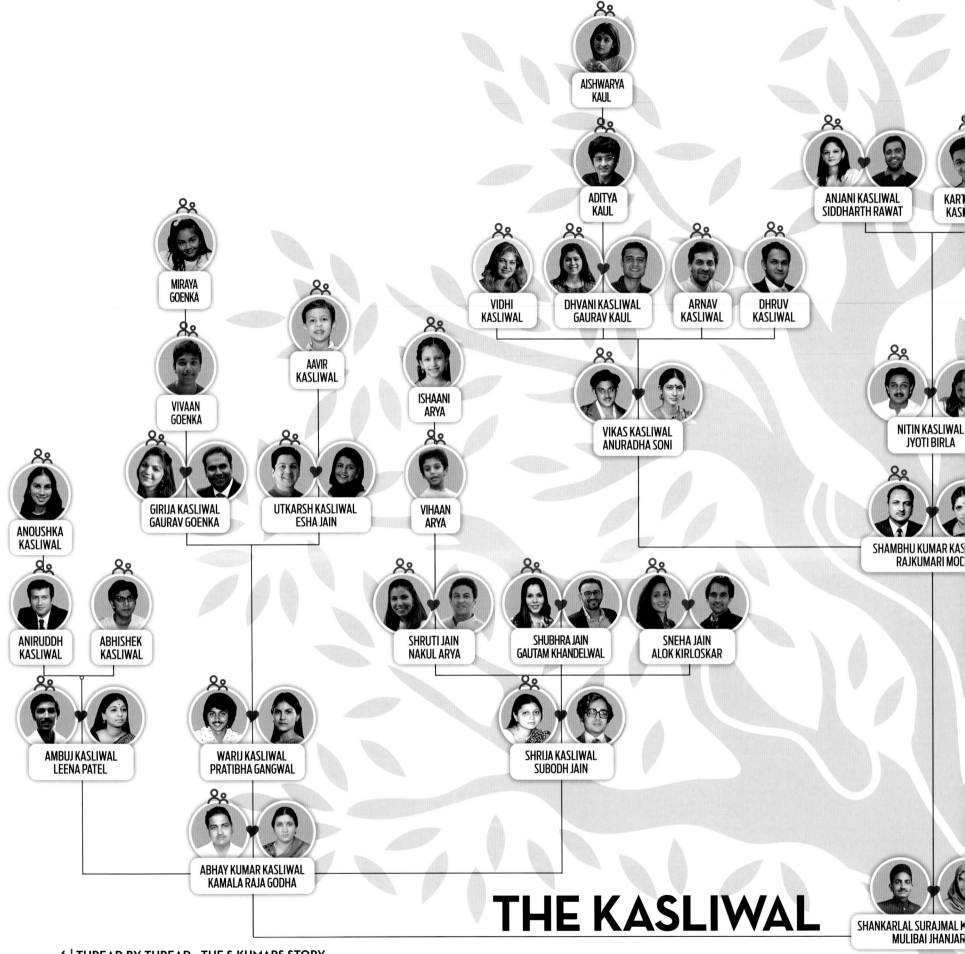

AISHWARYA KAUL

ADITYA KAUL

ANJANI KASLIWAL
SIDDHARTH RAWAT

KART
KAS

MIRAYA
GOENKA

AAVIR
KASLIWAL

ISHAANI
ARYA

VIDHI
KASLIWAL

DHVANI KASLIWAL
GAURAV KAUL

ARNAV
KASLIWAL

DHRUV
KASLIWAL

VIVAAN
GOENKA

ANOUSHKA
KASLIWAL

GIRIJA KASLIWAL
GAURAV GOENKA

UTKARSH KASLIWAL
ESHA JAIN

VIHAAN
ARYA

VIKAS KASLIWAL
ANURADHA SONI

NITIN KASLIWAL
JYOTI BIRLA

ANIRUDDH
KASLIWAL

ABHISHEK
KASLIWAL

SHAMBHU KUMAR KAS
RAJKUMARI MOD

SHRUTI JAIN
NAKUL ARYA

SHUBHRA JAIN
GAUTAM KHANDELWAL

SNEHA JAIN
ALOK KIRLOSKAR

AMBUJ KASLIWAL
LEENA PATEL

WARIJ KASLIWAL
PRATIBHA GANGWAL

SHRIJA KASLIWAL
SUBODH JAIN

ABHAY KUMAR KASLIWAL
KAMALA RAJA GODHA

THE KASLIWAL

SHANKARLAL SURAJMAL K
MULIBAI JHANJAR

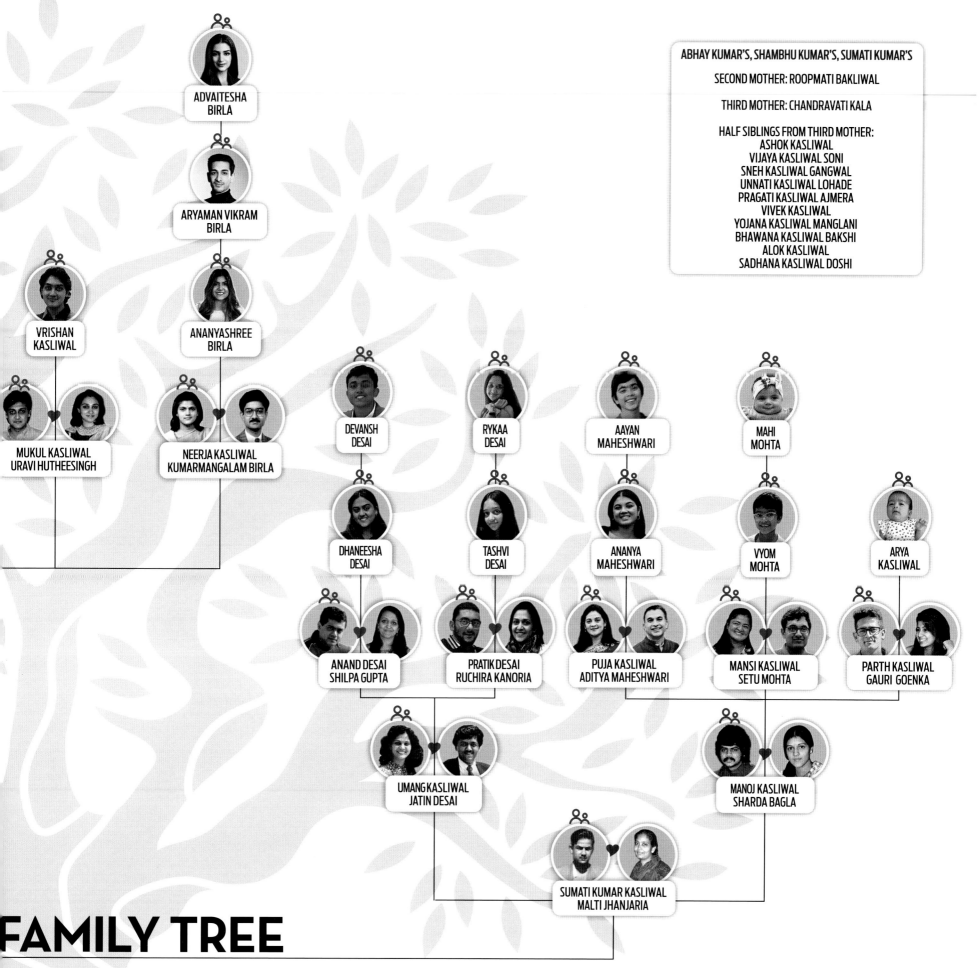

ADVAITESHA BIRLA

ARYAMAN VIKRAM BIRLA

VRISHAN KASLIWAL

ANANYASHREE BIRLA

MUKUL KASLIWAL
URAVI HUTHEESINGH

NEERJA KASLIWAL
KUMARMANGALAM BIRLA

DEVANSH DESAI

RYKAA DESAI

AAYAN MAHESHWARI

MAHI MOHTA

DHANEESHA DESAI

TASHVI DESAI

ANANYA MAHESHWARI

VYOM MOHTA

ARYA KASLIWAL

ANAND DESAI
SHILPA GUPTA

PRATIK DESAI
RUCHIRA KANORIA

PUJA KASLIWAL
ADITYA MAHESHWARI

MANSI KASLIWAL
SETU MOHTA

PARTH KASLIWAL
GAURI GOENKA

UMANG KASLIWAL
JATIN DESAI

MANOJ KASLIWAL
SHARDA BAGLA

SUMATI KUMAR KASLIWAL
MALTI JHANJARIA

FAMILY TREE

ABHAY KUMAR'S, SHAMBHU KUMAR'S, SUMATI KUMAR'S

SECOND MOTHER: ROOPMATI BAKLIWAL

THIRD MOTHER: CHANDRAVATI KALA

HALF SIBLINGS FROM THIRD MOTHER:
ASHOK KASLIWAL
VIJAYA KASLIWAL SONI
SNEH KASLIWAL GANGWAL
UNNATI KASLIWAL LOHADE
PRAGATI KASLIWAL AJMERA
VIVEK KASLIWAL
YOJANA KASLIWAL MANGLANI
BHAWANA KASLIWAL BAKSHI
ALOK KASLIWAL
SADHANA KASLIWAL DOSHI

CONTENTS

28 MADE IN HEAVEN
The most remarkable aspect of their marriage was the adventures that followed. As it happened, the honeymoon was spent driving from one place to another.

40 MATERIAL DREAMS
Quick to explore any new trail, Shambhu Kumar presented a sample to Bhau Saheb Apte who was piqued and interested.

12 NECTAR IN A SIEVE
Shambhu Kumar, the middle son, possibly might have found himself with neither the powers of the eldest nor the love reserved for the youngest. Yet, nothing could dampen the spunk he had been blessed with.

20 A DIAMOND FROM THE DUST
When the time seemed right, Shambhu Kumar decided to formalise the company. Bhau Saheb Apte came up with a canny suggestion.

46 A PLACE CALLED HOME
Though they did not seem to have a large social circle, the close-knit Kasliwal family was a world unto themselves.

54 A LEADER IS BORN
Shambhu Kumar can boast of countless employees who have been with the organisation for four or more decades, this is one of the most eloquent reflections of the success of a leader.

60 A RAGS TO RICHES STORY
Of simple stories about trust and support are great businesses built.

62 SIX YARDS OF FAME
In the history of Laxmi Vishnu Mills Shambhu Kumar would end up playing a key role. To him goes the credit for the huge success of the Terene sari.

66 RAMPING THINGS UP
Shambhu Kumar wanted to popularise synthetics as a more viable substitute and extend their distribution across India, including in the small towns and villages.

72 ORDER! ORDER!
With Filmi Mukkadama, S.Kumars struck gold! The thousands of postcards they received every week filled with appreciative messages was evidence of the show's success.

78 TURNING INDUSTRIALIST IN THE '70s
With S.Kumars being catapulted into a full-fledged textile manufacturing powerhouse, Shambhu Kumar was well on his way to becoming an industrialist.

84 THE ROTARY SPIRIT
Shambhu Kumar became a Rotarian in the true sense of the word. He would find in the service organisation, an echo of his own principles and values.

88 THE NATURE OF NURTURE
Today, none of the S.Kumars semi-skilled workers are lesser than their counterparts in other companies. Many of the current employees are second generation, who have joined the factory their fathers started in.

96 A TOUCH OF LOVE
A woman at the helm makes a difference, and Kaki's towelling factory is evidence of this. Her team considers their factory as their home.

100 SONS AS STAKEHOLDERS: STRENGTHS AND SKILLS
Shambhu Kumar could sense glory everywhere. It had been a total success. Full of name, kudos and acceptance throughout.

108 FRIEND, PHILOSOPHER AND GUIDE: A SON'S POINT OF VIEW
A bit of all three, that's what Shambhu Kumar has always been to Vikas, his eldest son.

112 HE IS AN ABSOLUTE ROCKSTAR: A SON'S TRIBUTE
To Nitin, his second son, Shambhu Kumar is a role model who people were and are in awe of.

116 EDUCATED, UNEDUCATED PARENTS: A SON SPEAKS
Mukul, Shambhu Kumar's youngest son, dedicated his Honours Degree to his parents.

120 EVERY PRINCIPLE OF LIFE I HAVE LEARNT IS FROM THEM: A DAUGHTER'S LOVE
Neerja, the baby of the family, has imbibed from her father the learning of not taking life too seriously.

124 LOOKING TO THE FUTURE
Kaka is watching, guiding, his hand on the rudder with the S.Kumars flag flying merrily in the winds of the future.

FOREWORD

"SOME OF THE WORLD'S GREATEST FEATS WERE ACCOMPLISHED BY PEOPLE NOT SMART ENOUGH TO KNOW THEY WERE IMPOSSIBLE."

As we were coming up on the 75th anniversary of S.Kumars, I began to wonder … What goes into seven and a half decades of a company's existence … in fact not just an existence, but a flourishing … This was a story worth telling and I set out on this assignment with this objective in mind … I wanted to pay homage to the achievements of my grandfather … S.Kumar of S.Kumars. And at the end of this enlightening journey … I am left with so much more regard and respect for my dearest Daddu …

To start at a time when stalwarts from Gujarat and Maharashtra stood as gatekeepers to the daunting textile industry … and to get a foot in the door with nothing except sheer determination and confidence … was a feat in itself.

What is awe-inspiring is that once Daddu entered, he never looked back. To move forward steadily and step-by-step took much dedication, acumen and attention to detail. He did it all happily and with panache. His commitment was infectious and it inspired all those around him to put in their heart and soul into building something long-lasting and worthwhile.

Once you achieve household recognition, it is very easy to lose your drive, but not so with my grandfather. He has a voracious appetite for ambition and an exceptional vigour to innovate and excel. He painstakingly thread-by-thread built an empire unlike any other. An industrialist with ideals, in today's day and age Daddu has all the makings of a relevant role model to all aspiring entrepreneurs, to influence them to go about their businesses with the highest of ethics and fair practices. This is the need of the hour, now more so than ever.

Our entire household was soaked with nostalgia while working on this project. It was so heart-warming to reconnect with senior team members and associates. And I can honestly say that each and every person we reached out to and spoke with had such fond memories of their time and relationship with S.Kumars. Daddu has pioneered such a force of products and people …

What is noteworthy is how my grandfather takes everything with a pinch of salt. His mantra is to never take anything seriously and always do everything sincerely. Through the ups and downs he has faced, he proclaims that he has never lost a single night's sleep over anything! On the contrary, he enjoyed the vicissitudes. He believes flatlining is never good and one must always keep moving.

As a granddaughter who loves her grandfather, I can't help but brim with joy and pride as his enterprise turns 75. It is not unexpected that I'd be full of praise for him, but I am fairly certain that as you read through the pages of this book, you will be transported to the transfixing adventure that he went on and you too will be full of admiration and reverence for the man I know as my grandfather.

The contributions and strides Daddu has made as an individual running his company in his chosen field for his country are incomparable. His career and life in textiles … it is not something to be trifled with. This is our gift … this is our legacy.

Vidhi

Vidhi Kasliwal

NECTAR IN A SIEVE

As a child, Shambhu Kumar made friends easily. And yet, in some way, he was a lonely child. His mother had died, tragically leaving behind him and his two brothers and Shambhu Kumar, the middle son, possibly might have found himself with neither the powers of the eldest, nor the love reserved for the youngest.

Yet, nothing in his circumstances could dampen the spunk he had been blessed with. A family story tells of how, when he was about four or five years old, he fell down the staircase and hurt himself quite badly. A lot of fuss and anxiety followed, but the boy bounced back. The spirit shone bright, negating any pain the fall may have gifted him with. And when someone asked him how he had managed to fall down, with a sportsmanship that would be a hallmark of his personality, the youngster offered to demonstrate exactly how he had fallen by tumbling down the steps again!

His father, Shankarlal Surajmal Kasliwal, B.Com, gold medallist in textile technology, was a trusted salesman for a textile mill in Amritsar where the family then lived. Though a busy man, he doted on his sons, calling them by pet names he would bestow on them. Sumati, the youngest, for one was often endearingly called Bhola.

And Abhay and Shambhu were Abhay Raja and Shambhu Raja; princes in their own right in his eyes.

Surprisingly, for those times, the father and sons had a free and open relationship, the boys could talk to him on anything, 'even taboo subjects,' to satisfy their curiosity. It helped allay the grief they felt over the death of their mother, whom they remembered as a beautiful woman with a soft voice, very spiritual in nature. In fact, Mulibai, which was her given name, inspired her husband to build a small Jain temple within the compound of their spacious family bungalow at 5120 Snehlataganj in Indore that he had bought years ago.

The spirituality that radiated from their mother would envelop all her children, guiding them through their life, in the years ahead, even long after she was gone.

But a travelling sales representative has to continuously travel. Knowing his job kept him away for days at a stretch, Shankarlal married again, a woman whom he hoped would look after his home and the three boys his first wife had presented him with. And now sanguine that his family was in safe hands again, he could pack his bags once more.

SHAMBHU KUMAR | IN 1939

It was not the best of times to grow up in India. There was an air of unrest, tumult all around.

India had launched itself into the freedom movement, and Lord Irwin, then the Viceroy of India appointed by King George V, had his hands full. In 1930, the year of Shambhu Kumar's birth, the Indian National Congress was already gaining strength and had taken history by the horns, declaring January 26 as the day for Poorna Swaraj, or complete independence.

The same year Sir C.V. Raman would win the Nobel Prize for Physics. Many Indians would read this as an affirmation that they could stand well on their own, and win, against the West in knowledge and learning. As if to highlight the fact that Indians could well chart their own destiny, Mohandas Karamchand Gandhi led his fellow countrymen into a cross-country march of open civil disobedience, as he strode purposefully across the 200 miles from the Sabarmati Ashram in Gujarat to Dandi to finally, at the end of 24 days on foot, pick up salt from the sea to protest the British monopoly on a substance so vital for life. Starting with 79 followers, he would have millions following him ... a comet's tail as he flew into the face of British law. The year-end would see the Indian leader boarding a ship for Round Table talks with the British rulers in London.

But, oblivious to all these events, that were spurring many movements that would change the destiny of his country, the young Shambhu Kumar did what many of his age did in an era when there was little beyond one's resources to occupy one's mind and time. He played with his brothers, attended school, and when his father moved to Calcutta, again as a salesperson, the family followed. He holds still, as one of his sharpest childhood memories, a strong remembrance of the

MULIBAI | 1928

place where his home was at 1 Pratap Ghosh Lane, Chittaranjan Avenue.

Of the three boys, it was Abhay Kumar and Shambhu Kumar who were really close. They would steal out from their school, Shree Vishuddhananda Saraswati Vidyalaya, to the K.C. Das shop at Dhurrumtollah, whose glass jars of sweets and trays of melt-in-the-mouth *rosogullas* beckoned so enticingly, and stuff themselves with *rosogullas*. The taste would linger on their tongues, smoothing away the scolding they would receive from their father when he discovered their escapade.

Perhaps the boys were too young to be buffeted by the fact that their step-mother had passed away and their father had married yet again, but other realities closed in, making them aware of the difficulties life could present even to the carefree.

The Second World War broke out, and India, as a part of a sovereign nation engaged in the hostilities, was forced to feel its heat.

When in September 1939, the British sent out 30000 Indians as part of the Allied push against the Nazis, the Quit India Movement followed as a huge nationwide protest against this high-handed measure. The war would give the Indian National Congress' movement for independence a huge thrust. It would also lead to shortages and suffering.

The war occupied everybody's mind. For those who had sons or brothers or husbands overseas, it held the persistent terror of bad news; for most others, it was a direct threat to life as they had known it. Shambhu Kumar remembers evenings spent listening to war news over the radio; about bombs that tore through western cities and thousands of soldiers and civilians dying on both sides, and jobs that were threatened by dwindling means. He would, prompted by patriotism, launch his own initiative towards the freedom movement. Inspired by the in-depth conversations with maternal cousin Vimalchand Jhanjari, a well-respected correspondent of the Times of India, in Indore, Shambhu Kumar would work closely with the social reformer, Dr. S.N. Subba Rao of Bangalore, to start the Congress Sewa Dal in Indore, in Independent India.

As history proved, some would grow rich during the war; and some would become very poor. To avoid facing the possibility of finding himself in the second category, Shankarlal decided to find a safer haven.

By the time the war ended, the Kasliwal family decided to shift back to Indore, where they originally belonged.

Life in Indore provided a kind of sanctuary for Shambhu Kumar. He was enrolled in the reputed Trilokchand Jain Higher Secondary School. His father, hoping to find fresh pastures and put his academic learning to good use, made up his mind to stretch his horizons.

As there were more mouths to feed, Shankarlal decided to make a fresh bid to make his fortune. The city of gold beckoned.

Once he reached Bombay, family in tow, Shankarlal joined the Seksaria Cotton Mills. Even before World War II had begun, India was the second largest producer of textiles in the world.

Shankarlal would operate from near the Crawford Market, where everything from fruits and vegetables to goods imported from England were sold. He set up his home nearby, taking a place in Khattar Galli, near the Cowasjee Patel water tank that was one of the reservoirs that supplied water to the city.

GATEWAY OF INDIA, BOMBAY

AS A CHILD, I WAS NOT NAUGHTY, I WAS MISCHIEVOUS. AND THOUGH I WAS A STUDIOUS STUDENT, I WAS NOT A SHARP ONE; I HAVE NO DEGREES BUT LOTS OF LEARNING.

– SHAMBHU KUMAR

FROM MY FATHER I LEARNT TO NEVER GIVE UP AND I WOULD LIKE TO TEACH THIS TO MY CHILDREN, GRANDCHILDREN AND GREAT-GRANDCHILDREN.

– SHAMBHU KUMAR

Back in the years of the World War, Shankarlal grappled with the fact that it had caused serious upsets in the cloth business. By 1943 the government had taken over textiles as an essential commodity, along with food grains. Yet with a quota of 19-20 bales, he managed to earn a neat profit. He would now sow the profits into a venture that he hoped would reap a rich harvest.

Thus, in 1944, he managed to set up a shop for textiles. He worked hard at building his business, keeping his family comfortable in new premises at 41/42 Champa Galli near Zaveri Bazaar.

Eager to spread further, he quickly opened 8 or 9 branches all over India. He had a business partner, his mother's cousin, Ratanlal ji Patni.

Relationships in business were relatively informal in those days. There was no cut throat competition. Merchants, even rivals, could be asked for help. With a helping hand here, and another there, by end of 1944, shops bearing the board, 'Surajmal and Sons Pvt. Ltd.' were buying fabrics and selling to customers across the country. It was all done with élan. Letterheads with the company name were printed, and letters would fly across the country as a way of communicating business news.

Perhaps Shankarlal had settled more for show than substance; not realising that a business needs to be built brick by brick to stand strong as a lasting edifice. The rash of flashy stores did not bring in the expected returns, stocks moved slowly, money stayed locked up and debts mounted. Within a year-and-a-half since he had floated his enterprise, it was all over.

Shankarlal, with his family, returned home. His dreams broken-winged.

Not quite, though, for ambition reared its head once again, whispering stories of riches waiting to be plucked like fruit from a tree.

He toyed with the idea of starting in another direction. His children would listen wide-eyed as he talked about new paths he could walk on in business. It seemed to matter little that destiny placed hurdles in his way; his spirit was buoyant, and his mind teemed with possibilities.

It was a rare attitude, this never-say-die approach to life; and Shankarlal may have not known it then, but it would kindle in his sons a desire to fulfil their father's destiny and dreams.

Now embarked on a new mission, Shankarlal decided to refurbish the Ashok Cloth Mills in Rewa, putting his knowledge of machines and textile production to good use. With great enthusiasm, he bought land, the machines were procured, and the Mill would have run smoothly indeed, fired by Shankarlal's enthusiastic vision, had it not been for the severe shortages that followed the end of the War. Shankarlal returned to Indore. His dreams he packed away and pushed deep into some dark recess of his cupboard.

The worst of his fears had come to pass. But he kept his family afloat, never letting the children know of the troubles that faced him; of the struggle to keep them in the comfort they had grown up knowing. In fact, when his elder son, Abhay Kumar's wedding was fixed to Kamala Raja, a girl from a well-heeled family, Shankarlal decided that he would do his *Samadhis* proud. Seriously

strapped for money, he had to borrow from 'every nook and corner' even to be able to pay for the '*baraat*.' Shambhu Kumar remembers borrowing from an affluent Sindhi shop-owner in the Cloth Market at Indore, Sunderdas ji, 5,000 rupees, quite a princely sum at that time. He would repay this amount 2 or 3 years later.

Astutely, Shambhu Kumar realised the truth of their situation, the family was coming face to face with penury.

The great World War II had ended in 1945. But India, though not directly scarred by the War, was still fighting its own battles for freedom. Indians realised that none of the benefits of the British winning the war would be passed on to them. Shortages continued as the British focussed on rebuilding cities devastated by the war. And the growing intensity of the Freedom Struggle, with the entire nation adopting Gandhi's messages of Swarajya and non-violence in its way, now motivated Shambhu Kumar to find his own independence.

Alerting his elder brother Abhay Kumar to the fact that it was their duty to take on some of the burden of the family on themselves, he made a plan to help them take things in hand. They should go to Bombay. Find a means to earn and support the family

But when the time came to leave, Shambhu Kumar, on second thoughts told his brother, who had dutifully got married just a few months earlier not to uproot himself. Determined to try his fortune in the city, the younger brother took the plunge.

He would go alone to Bombay.

Shambhu Kumar was 17. And the large, unknown city waited for him. ⑤

A DIAMOND
FROM THE DUST

The year was 1946. The teeming crowds at the Victoria Terminus in Bombay where the train deposited Shambhu Kumar did not quite faze him as it had many others walking its platforms for the first time. Perhaps he spent a few minutes within the giant hall of the concourse, taking in the arches and the fluted columns that held the ceiling aloft. From outside, the station presented an even more awe-inspiring sight, as it stood outlined against the city's blue sky. The three-dimensional carvings of local animal and plant species, the roundels with human faces, and the meshed lattices of stone that decorated the rose windows bore witness to the intensity of thought and work that had gone into the structure's creation. A testimony to the Gothic history of architecture, the building had wedded Indian motifs and decorations with Western gargoyles to create a unique memorial to Anglo-Indian workmanship. Best represented by the two columns, one topped by the lion of England and the other by a very Indian Bengal tiger.

But, bent as he was on finding his refuge in the vast city he had arrived in, the young man hurried on. He knew his destination. A building located in the busy area known as Vithalwadi in Kalbadevi. It was a short walk from the station, and so, he set off on foot. As he moved along the narrow streets, lined with buildings standing shoulder to shoulder on either side, the salt of the city's sea breeze swirled around his senses. The humid air added beads of sweat to his brow, but his eyes blazed with determination and expectations

of the future. Already, as the train had rattled through the distance from Indore to Bombay, its sharp whistle warning man and cattle away from its tracks, the boy had made a plan to join the cloth business. To buy and sell cloth, taking small steps to start him on his way.

Hand carts piled with peanuts and fruits, men hawking trinkets strung on to bamboo frames on poles, roadside cobblers, and shops with goldsmiths bending over small flames as they pounded on ornaments with tiny hammers met his eyes. Dodging the flowing mass of humanity, he turned into the street where he would find his room on the second floor of a building. This had been the office of Surajmal and Sons. It would be his base now for the business ventures he had in mind.

The space, though small, would have a lasting role to play in Shambhu Kumar's career. He would treasure it as the only tangible legacy passed on by his father.

The goodwill of the father reached out to help the young entrepreneur. One of Shankarlal's connections agreed to help. He suggested Shambhu Kumar buy material and give it to him to sell, as he had contacts among buyers. And that set the ball rolling.

To begin with, 'I would get 15 bales for 15000 and sell for 15000, making zilch off the lot,' Shambhu Kumar says. Though he had almost no capital, with an uncanny ability to make riches out of waste, Shambhu Kumar sold hessian gunny sacks, the jute wrappings that his cloth bundles were delivered in. And slowly he would increase the quantity of his purchase. Little by little, literally an anna or two at a time, he was building his capital.

Once, Shambhu Kumar had collected enough reserves, though small, he

OLD KALBADEVI BOMBAY

> # TAKE ADVICE BUT USE YOUR OWN BRAINS. WHATEVER YOU DO, 70 PER CENT OF THE PEOPLE ARE GOING TO CRITICISE YOU. TAKE EVERYTHING IN YOUR STRIDE.
> ### – SHAMBHU KUMAR

SHAMBHU KUMAR | BOMBAY | 1948

planned to move ahead. And there was more luck awaiting him.

The simplest of events can have mammoth consequences. When a broker, Narayandas ji Shrikishan, impressed by the earnest way in which Shambhu Kumar talked about business, offered to introduce him to the sole selling agent for a prominent mill, none of the three imagined the simple offer held the seed of events that would change destinies and build fortunes.

Laxman Vaman Apte or Bhau Saheb as he was respectfully called, was a businessman of means. His father, Vaman Shridhar Apte, also known as Tatya Saheb, had come to Bombay as a young man, sent there to train in the cloth business, having had to forgo further education due to ill-health. Tatya was a matriculate. He apprenticed himself as a trainee in a cloth shop, in what must be the world's largest cloth market, the Mulji Jetha Market, commonly referred to as the MJ Market, in South Bombay.

Tatya had quickly learned the ropes of trading in textiles, and impressed his mentor Vallabhdas Jairam by setting up his own cloth business. Soon, he was an established cloth merchant, causing heads to turn when he walked into the market in his dhoti and shirt with a long coat or *dagla* over it, and a small *pugree* on his head, to take his place in his *pedhi*, and conduct the day's business. Within two decades of his coming to Bombay, Tatya had secured the prize of being the sole selling agent for Kohinoor Mills, which was owned by the British firm, Killick Nixon and Company. He started earning a commission for every piece of cloth he sold for the Mill. He would hold that position in the industry for 51 years. The Mill had three units, based in different locations, while two units produced varied qualities of cloth and yarn, the third one was dedicated to producing artificial silk and other synthetic cloth.

The Aptes had their shop, or *pedhi*, as it was called, in a prominent corner of the market. Like most of the *pedhis* in the market, it was furnished only with white mattresses and roll cushions for the men to lean against. A *gumastha* would sit writing accounts, usually in Gujarati, using a reed pen that was dipped in a bottle of ink after every few words, to keep the ink flowing. A small container of sand was always at hand, to be sprinkled on the page to blot the excess ink and prevent smudging. Apte's shop proclaimed its prosperity through the existence of a mezzanine floor and a ladder to reach it. A safe stood solidly at the deep end of the cubicle.

At the time that Shambhu Kumar met Laxman Vaman Apte, who looked after the technical aspects of his father's business, the latter had acquired all the luxuries a rich and prosperous man awards himself with. A small fleet of cars, a bungalow to house his family, and membership in the prestigious Willingdon Club near the Mahalakshmi race course. He also had a formidable phalanx of dealers and agents taking his business forward.

Apte saw in Shambhu Kumar a reflection of his father. Shambhu too had been forced by circumstance to curtail his studies, thanks to having to shuttle through four schools and complete his matriculation privately. But Apte saw the same curiosity, the same fire of ambition to make a success of his business burning through Shambhu's eyes, that had once burned in his father, Tatya Saheb. Later, in an interview, Shambhu Kumar would say about the budding relationship with Bhau Saheb, 'It was my good fortune that he felt that I had promise and should be guided and supported.'

Apte gave the fledgling businessman cloth from Kohinoor Mills to sell. Contemporaries from that time remember the young Shambhu Kumar standing in front of the Bombay Dyeing shop in Zaveri Bazaar and selling his burden of cloth to them. He was a committed salesman, having imbibed some of his father's astonishing salesmanship.

As the relationship with Bhau Saheb grew, Shambhu Kumar was quick to imbibe the qualities he noticed in his mentor too. Whatever the circumstance, the company dealt with it, only with honesty. Apte never sold in black, though due to the shortages of cloth and quotas set up in the aftermath of independence, the temptation was huge, thanks to an unceasing demand. He inculcated the same values in his sons, and

Shambhu Kumar learnt too, watching the older man at work. Honesty in business would be his guiding principle through the years ahead.

Within six months of living in Bombay, Shambhu Kumar persuaded his elder brother to move to the city. Abhay Kumar brought his family along. Bhau Saheb guided the brothers, who would meet him every morning before they started their workday.

Shambhu Kumar would often join the older man for an early morning game of squash at the Cricket Club of India (CCI), where Apte had recommended Shambhu Kumar for a membership. The day would be spent at the Shop for trade and a visit to the Mill. More often than not, the brothers would drop in again to visit Apte in the evening, at his bungalow, Woodlands on Peddar Road. Discussions on business would follow.

When the time seemed right, Shambhu Kumar decided to formalise the company. Apte came up with a canny suggestion.

Shambhu Kumar was to start a proprietorship. When Bhau Saheb suggested it be named as S.Kumar and Company. Thus, it was that S.Kumars came into being, on Janmashtami Day, with a puja attended by Apte and his family too, in the modest Vithalwadi office. The year was 1948.

Later on, it would become a partnership firm, with Abhay Kumar, R.S. Kharkar and Bhau Saheb's elder son-in-law, Kamalakar Modak, joining Shambhu Kumar as partners.

Apte encouraged his protegee to try exploring new avenues in cloth. He pointed him toward Kohinoor Mill number 3, the one that created synthetic materials. Determined to make the most of what he perceived as a challenge, Shambhu Kumar decided to buy

SHAMBHU KUMAR & BROTHERS WITH BHAU SAHEB

ABHAY KUMAR | IN 1952

SHAMBHU KUMAR | IN 1950

SUMATI KUMAR | IN 1939

IMAGE COURTESY: PASTINDIA.COM

TURNING BACK IS AN OPTION FOR SOMEONE WHO HAS SOMEWHERE TO GO BACK TO. YOU MUST KEEP GOING ON. DON'T WITHDRAW.

– SHAMBHU KUMAR

and sell a product that was not a fast moving one. When he realised that he could get no credit from Apte, he devised his own method of creating a turnover of cash.

Shambhu Kumar would give a crossed cheque when picking up goods. He would pack the goods and take them to MJ Market, where he had connected with a handful of dealers. He would sell them at a small profit, take a bearer cheque for what he had sold and deposit it into his account. It was a fool-proof method, for he never defaulted and could keep the turnover growing with little risk involved. Thinking back on the time when he would sell the jute packing material as scrap, he would say he had learnt the value of 'never to look down on any honest source of income.'

S.Kumars had reached into the future, starting practically from scratch and now growing speedily and steadily. From being buyers and sellers, the brothers were now officially dealers. Along with the dealership of Kohinoor Mills, they were selling agents for an entire battery of other flourishing plants: Ellichpur Cotton Mills near Nagpur, Shree Ram Silks in Rishra, near Calcutta, Madura Mills in Ambasamudram, Madurai and Ramesh Silk Mills in Surat.

Shambhu Kumar was now officially supporting his family, still living in Indore. He was a generous provider. Younger brother, Sumati Kumar, remembers that while a student at the Daly College, he had written to Shambhu 'Dada' for a cricket bat and ball. 'He sent 100 rupees, a very generous sum at that time, and I bought a Lesley Ames bat, which was considered among the best. Today the same bat costs 16000 rupees, so you can understand the value of it then.'

On Bhau Saheb Apte's advice the brothers shifted to a three-room cottage just in front of his house. They moved from the one-room tenement that had offered only the privacy of a curtain drawn to divide the single room in half and a balcony in which they would cook, into the more spacious accommodation on Peddar Road, near the stately Villa Theresa High School

The cottage would soon accommodate 11 souls, with Sumati Kumar and his family who had by now joined his older brothers, Abhay Kumar's family, and maternal uncle Nihalchand ji Bakliwal, plus a childhood friend of Shambhu Kumar all sharing the space; but intent of the business of growing his business, Shambhu Kumar did not seem to feel inconvenienced in any way. Living in a joint family had taught him and his brothers to be accommodating. More significant was the fact that the days of early struggle to establish themselves and manage with meagre meals like just rice with salt were well behind the brothers. And the road ahead seemed strewn with flowers.

To Apte it must have seemed he was watching history repeating itself, as Shambhu Kumar grew his business methodically and systematically. By 1954 he had the dealership of many mills in hand. And was so successful at his business that mills would approach S.Kumars to take their cloth.

Slowly but surely, working with the assiduousness of an ant collecting grain, Shambhu Kumar continued on his mission. And all through, he kept in mind one simple tenet. Learnt from Bhau Saheb. Never to let go of his principles, never to indulge in falsehood nor in business practices that would hurt others. ◉

MADE IN HEAVEN

Both Shambhu Kumar's brothers, older and younger than him, had already settled into married life. Shambhu Kumar, who had spent the past few years setting up his business finally felt it was his turn to set up his own home.

In 1955, at the 'advanced' age of 25 years, Shambhu Kumar donned the role of a family man. It was, as was the norm in most traditional families, an arranged match.

Rajkumari Modi was all of 13 years old. She was studying in class eight, and though the schooling was in Hindi, had studied English till class four. The Modi and Kasliwal families were known to each other for many years. When the fathers of the to-be bride and the prospective groom decided they would bind their children in matrimony, the Kasliwal family paid a visit to formalise things.

However, Shambhu Kumar did not, as many sons did, meekly accept the idea of stepping into married life without knowing his prospective partner's mind. He insisted that her opinion be asked, was she agreeable to accepting him as a husband. 'Ask her consent,' he prompted his family, and they obliged. Rajkumari Kasliwal remembers that she loudly proclaimed, 'yes,' a word that still brings a fond smile to her husband's lips, though she was not really sure what it entailed. The formal engagement followed, and a date was fixed for the wedding.

Shambhu Kumar found himself being drawn into a whirlpool of emotions as he waited for the day when the young woman would stand by his side as his wife. Letters would fly to and fro, and in one daring escapade Rajkumari responded to her fiancé's request that she meet him on the terrace. A photograph from that meeting shows the two shy young people posing for the camera.

The wedding itself was a simple affair. When the girl's family asked about the *dahej* expected, in keeping with the *riwaj* of those days, the

RAJKUMARI WEDS SHAMBHU KUMAR 1955

MEN AND WOMEN ARE NOT EQUAL, I FEEL WOMEN
ARE MUCH BETTER. EVEN AT SETTING UP BUSINESSES,
THEIR MINDS CONSOLIDATE.

– SHAMBHU KUMAR

groom's family accepted a single rupee and a coconut, in deference to tradition, and the *baraat* set off from the Sheesh Mahal close by, to the bride's house where the ceremony was held.

Perhaps the most remarkable aspect of Shambhu Kumar's marriage, was the adventures that followed. As it happened, it was decided to spend the honeymoon driving from one place to another.

It was no ordinary road trip. The newlyweds drove a newly bought Hillman, and a close childhood friend of the groom, Narsinghdas Gupta and his wife and their two children accompanied them. The men took turns at the wheel, and with amazing zest, they covered 8000 miles through three months of non-stop sightseeing, stopping the nights in quaint Dak Bungalows that were available in the towns they visited. They took boat rides, got their clothes washed, ate the local cuisine of the states they passed through. It was not an expensive trip by any standards. Rooms cost two rupees a night, and they would take two rooms, of course.

There were times when, Rajkumari, chaffing at being relegated to the back seat instead of by her brand new husband's side, would feign motion sickness and move to sit in front. It was all part of a wilful new bride's way of getting to know the man she had married. They discovered each other and India's true heart in the process.

Narsingh Gupta remembers that when they stopped on the way back at Shirdi to fill petrol in their car, the man at the petrol pump came up holding a single chappal. It was the same one that had got left behind earlier during their way in.

In Madras, Narendra Chettiyar, a big dealer for Kohinoor Mills for the South, made them feel very welcome, hosting

SHAMBHU KUMAR & RAJKUMARI WITH FIRST-BORN | JUHU BEACH | 1957

SHAMBHU KUMAR WITH SON VIKAS

RAJKUMARI BEHIND THE WHEEL

KASLIWAL & MODI FAMILY TIES | SHANKARLAL & MULIBAI (3RD FROM LEFT) | RATANLAL MODI (3RD FROM RIGHT)

them. They watched the ice skating show in Delhi, and in Calcutta they were encouraged to take time off to watch the Test Match by local dealers who also organised food for the day. Shambhu Kumar however, let his friend and the wives enjoy the match, while he set off to the market to squeeze in some business.

Back in Bombay, the couple shared space in the three-room cottage with Abhay Kumar, Sumati Kumar and their respective families. And the house was open and welcoming to all. Rajkumari's experiences in her maternal home of both affluence and a much reduced economic status due to business downturns had made her aware of the need to be thrifty and she learnt to adjust quickly. It would hone Rajkumari's housekeeping skills very quickly. A year later, she returned to her mother's house, deep in the interior of Madhya Pradesh, to bear the first of her children, Vikas. Three others would follow over the next 15 years, Nitin, Mukul and Neerja.

It was while the couples lived together at Nalanda Cottage that the nomenclature 'Kaka' and 'Kaki' were tagged on to Shambhu Kumar and Rajkumari. The older children called their father 'Pappa' and mother 'Mummy,' and Shambhu Kumar's children followed their cousins' example. No one felt it was necessary to change this, or correct them. The bond between the brothers made it quite immaterial. Abhay was the perfect foil to Shambhu, cool versus hot-headedness. And it was Abhay Kumar who named all the new-borns and also made it a point to attend the school functions of all the children without discrimination. It is interesting to note that he named most of the children in synonyms of Kamala, his wife's name: Ambuj, Warij, Shrija, Neerja. All of which stand for the lotus.

Rajkumari adapted to life in the metropolis easily enough. She taught her children their

ROAD TRIP | 1955

THREE BROTHERS WITH THEIR WIVES & FAMILY

ONE SHOULD TREAT ONE'S WIFE AS AN EQUAL SO AS TO GET EQUAL AMOUNT OF RESPECT. MY WIFE IS AND ALWAYS HAS BEEN MY BIGGEST STRENGTH.

– SHAMBHU KUMAR

NEWLYWEDS MANDU 1955

MY HUSBAND KEPT EVERYONE HAPPY WITH A SMILE ON HIS FACE. NO ONE COULD READ HIS WORRIES EVER.

– RAJKUMARI KASLIWAL

lessons, her knowledge of English standing her in good stead. Later, when the children grew old enough to spend long hours studying on their own for the exams, she would knit while they burnt the midnight oil. With her husband away most of the day, Rajkumari spent time with her brothers-in-law, learning to play squash, cricket and carrom, among other games.

Rajkumari remembers how the small family held together. Vikas would stand outside waiting for his father to come home from work. Shambhu Kumar would teach her to drive, shunting their car up and down the slope to the cottage. In an expression of what can only be called delicately romantic, he would also take her out to buy glass bangles just because she loved them or come home carrying her favourite *chana* snack wrapped in newspaper from a shop in Vithalwadi.

Though she learnt driving a year after her marriage, Rajkumari would get her licence only when Vikas was old enough for school. Then, nothing could stop her. By 1958, she was zooming around shopping for vegetables, dropping and picking up the children from school, taking off on long drives. Driving would grow into a passion. And when the family went on the extended pilgrimage drives that would be a regular part of their yearly activities, Shambhu Kumar would share the driving with his wife, sitting stoically and sanguine, as she pushed the accelerator and kept the speedometer steady at 100. Those who watch her drive, marvel at her steady hand and eye and the spirit of a racing car driver that would make her take off like a jet. Rajkumari admits that to-date she is 'like one possessed once behind the wheel,' and regardless of whether it is a Maruti or a Mercedes, she enjoys the feel of a car in her hands.

Of her role as Shambhu Kumar's wife, Rajkumari says that she only wanted to see him happy. Her happiness, she avers, is dependent on his.

Most people who have known the couple swear that their life together is a template for an ideal marriage. Neither is seen without the other; where one goes, the other goes too. They share the same interests, and bestow the same degree of warmth and care on family, friends and those in their employ.

And through the years, it is to his wife's calm demeanour that the famous Shambhu Kumar temper that would make him flare up like a firecracker has been tamed.

Not always, though, according to an anecdote shared by his wife. 'I got angry too,' she recounted, 'when he tore up the tickets.' This rare occurrence was in fact justified, as the mother was keen they accompany their first-born when he went to Boston to join the MBA programme at Harvard. But Shambhu Kumar was neck deep in work, there was no way he could tear himself away to make the long trip. And when his wife pushed hard, he simply tore up the tickets.

Through the nearly 70 years of their togetherness, such incidents as the one above, have been few and far in between. The 'love birds,' as they have often been referred to, have a deep regard and respect for each other and need no words to understand what the other wants. It was indeed a match made in heaven on that Basant Panchami day, on January 28, 1955. ⑤

MATERIAL
DREAMS

Cloth as India knew it was going to undergo a transformation. Cotton and silk had been staple products and Gandhi had added the more homespun khadi to create a new apparel vocabulary.

Then came a new entrant on the textile scene. Terylene.

The cloth that would, over the years ahead, take S.Kumars to new heights, originated in a chemical laboratory. As early as the 1930s, a material that was called polyester plastic was discovered in a DuPont lab. An American scientist, W.H. Carothers used it as a stepping stone to work on his discovery, Nylon.

The scientific world went agog with the possibilities this man-made creation could open up. In 1941, British scientists, J.R. Whinfield and J.T. Dickson experimented further, taking Carothers' work to the next level. In time, they patented what we know as PET. The two scientists went on to develop the first ever polyester fibre. They named it Terylene.

A British company, the Imperial Chemical Industries, would be the first to produce this new wonder fabric. DuPont, in America, would start production of polyester too, under the brand name Dacron.

Advertisements to popularise the material included a claim that said it was, 'a miracle fibre that can be worn for 68 days without ironing, and still look presentable.' Terylene was water resistant, and the fibre was strong enough to withstand repetitive movements with minimal wear and tear. Besides it boasted of being shrink resistant, and did not stain or stretch. The fact that it did not crease or wrinkle made it attractive to housewives, who could find in the fabric a release from long drawn out struggles with a heavy iron and crushed shirts and trousers. Cheaper than natural fabrics to produce, it was a high return on investment to producer and seller, in turn.

Far away from the country where it had first made its appearance, Terylene would create magic for both Apte and his protegee. In fact, it would be the key that would open S.Kumars' fortunes, setting the company on its path to becoming one of the biggest and most durable players in the textile business.

Ram Gopal ji Neema, who had stepped in to help Shambhu Kumar at the start of his career, was destined to repeat the gesture. He was one of the dealers in nylon. Ram Gopal ji happened to be the maternal uncle of Shambhu Kumar's friend, Narsingh Gupta. The two spent a lot of time discussing work, among other things, and Narsingh remembers advising his friend to

pick up nylon, as it 'sold very well.' And at two paise a metre, it was cheap.

Quick to explore any new trail, Shambhu Kumar presented a sample to Apte who was piqued and interested.

Shambhu Kumar then approached Imperial Chemical Industries. With uncanny business sense, he presented to them the future they could enjoy if they would supply to Kohinoor Mills. Impressed by his clear thinking and foresight, the principals of ICI agreed easily enough. A supply and demand chain was forged thus, between ICI and Kohinoor Mills, with Shambhu Kumar acting as the vital link.

Soon after the introduction, Kohinoor Mills started buying the polyester fibre from the Imperial Chemical Industries and spinning it, to weave into cloth. The material was then duly processed to make it friendly to skin. Cotton fibre would be blended in with the synthetic fibre at the yarn stage, to ensure the end product would be of a fine, fluid quality. At other times, the two fibres would get integrated in the loom, at the weaving stage. It depended on what the cloth was being made for and the pricing it could command.

And S.Kumars became the sole selling agent for this new synthetic blend. Selling material that the Kohinoor Mill number 3 wove only as per Shambhu Kumar's specification. For a man who was not part of the company, it was a huge recognition indeed, of his knowledge of the market. Though Khatau Mills entered as a Terylene manufacturer a few months later, Kohinoor had first entry advantage and S.Kumars would benefit from that fact.

Shambhu Kumar did his bit to ensure quick sales of the innovative fabric. He broke marketing conventions and went not only to wholesalers but also to semi-wholesalers and developed alliances with them. To further fire the wholesalers into efficient sales, he set up a scheme that he titled the Prompt Payment Discount. The discount on goods would depend on whether payment came in within 10 days, 30 days, or 60 days. On the flip side, he wove in a penalty for delays that could be termed 'intentional.' Of course, if the problem was genuine, he would treat the man like a 'wounded soldier,' and solve it.

Soon, 'Bhaiya Saheb' as he was called in those days, (because he called his brother Dada Saheb) was not only respected in the marketplace for his business acumen, but as someone you could approach for a fair hearing if a problem should arise. Little wonder, Shambhu Kumar had almost no defaults in payments to worry about.

Kohinoor launched the blended fabric as suiting material. Measuring 28-29 inches (approximately

71 cms) in width, it was a precursor to the uniform material that would become the S.Kumars hallmark, and the market took to it quickly. Profits of 25-35 per cent were realised. The path ahead was shining with promise.

Shambhu Kumar would 'partner' with yet another British company. But that was way in the future.

To some extent the protegee was now showing his mentor the way ahead. Astutely understanding the process of weaving, Shambhu Kumar would, through the next decades, experiment with and fix the number of threads for weaving different blended fabrics, like gabardine and matte cloth.

The ICI developed a certain confidence in Shambhu Kumar that was reflected in

MULJI JETHA MARKET | BOMBAY

the actions of their Indian counterpart, Chemicals and Fibres of India. For years to come S.Kumars would develop an extensive business being the exclusive dealer of CAFI's export surplus that included excellent quality ready-made shirts, suitings and crepe ladies wear material.

In fact, it was Ramesh Singhal of CAFI who made introductions between Shambhu Kumar and Vilas and Viraj Nath Singh of Ahmed Woollen Mills. And together they forayed into light weight woollens, another precursor of things to come decades later.

It was also in the later part of the next decade, that Shambhu Kumar would experiment with acrylic and introduce it into suitings as 'Polyacron,' a blend of polyester, viscose and acrylic.

Acknowledged today as the pioneer who created innovative blends in cloth produced in India, Shambhu Kumar's weaving systems are the norm followed by most mills even today. And the shade card that he created back then, remains an industry norm even now, in many mills across India.

The reputation of both S.Kumars, the company and Shambhu Kumar, the man was steadily growing. Almost every textile market in every part of India was familiar with the company by now, as cloth merchants one could trust.

When Madura Mills approached S.Kumars for help in selling their

THE THREE SONS | VIKAS, NITIN, MUKUL

YOU RETIRE ONLY WHEN YOU RETIRE, UNTIL THEN YOU DO WHAT YOU CAN. I AM AN AMBITIOUS MAN EVEN TODAY; AND MY AMBITION IS TO BE HAPPY.

– SHAMBHU KUMAR

SHAMBHU KUMAR

BOTH BROTHERS WITH MADHAV RAO APTE

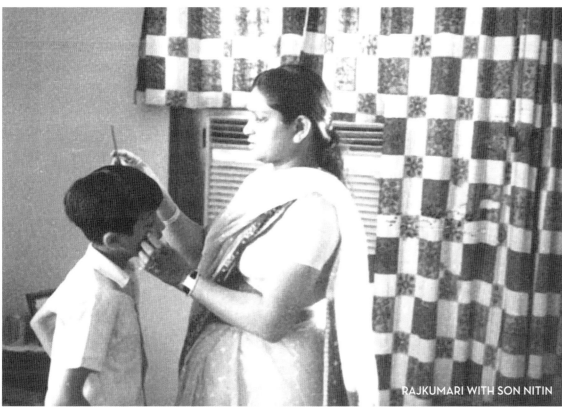

RAJKUMARI WITH SON NITIN

product, Shambhu Kumar bought the entire suiting material on an exclusive basis. The material would reach the market, and buyers would find the legend S.Kumars running along the selvedge of the entire fabric. It was a name they could trust.

Knowing the importance of branding almost instinctively, Shambhu Kumar had Nishikant Shirodkar design the logo that would hopefully make the brand a household name.

Perhaps it was while he was watching his sons get ready for school that the idea struck him. Despite the fact that the uniforms were washed everyday and ironed before wearing, they looked so much the worse for wear by afternoon. The boisterous school day with playtime roughhousing had a devastating effect. Changing the neatly turned out boys who left home in well ironed uniforms into rough and tumble scallywags on their return.

Perhaps, uniforms made of blended material would wear better. And be easier to maintain too.

Quick to accept Shambhu Kumar's idea, Kohinoor Mills sent out material for school uniforms in polyester-cotton blends. The idea caught on quickly enough, demand grew, not just from schools, but also other organisations where uniforms were a requirement for personnel.

On the home front, changes were required too.

By 1960 the family was ready to move into more comfortable accommodation. They had both the will and the means to do so. Padam, a building that cornered the crossroad of Peddar Road and Gamadia Road where it turned left into Warden Road, was the chosen location. The family would shift out from the cottage to a place where they could find ample space to let their dreams fly free. ◉

A PLACE CALLED HOME

The 1960s were a significant decade in Indian history. The country was experiencing a change of guard necessitated by the death of India's first prime minister, Jawaharlal Nehru. India's third prime minister, Lal Bahadur Shastri floated the 'Jai Jawan Jai Kisan' slogan, giving focus to the two vital points: defence and food for all, and respect for those involved in both areas. Two other significant milestones included the fact that Indira Gandhi became the country's first woman prime minister, and in 1966, yet another businessman, Dhiralal Champak Ambani would plant his flag on the textile scene by launching Reliance Industries. A 350 sq ft room with a table, three chairs and a telephone would be the first office of the Reliance Commercial Corporation at Narsee Natha Street in Masjid Bunder, almost mirroring the S.Kumars office in Vithalwadi, and the offices of many other fledgling enterprises of that time.

But none of this had a direct impact on the Kasliwal family. Even as Shambhu Kumar pushed his frontiers further and further to expand his business, his vaulting ambition balanced by ground values lighting the way ahead, he ensured his family was cocooned from any turbulence that might shake the outside world.

Panna Kiran Javeri remembers it all vividly. The 16-year-old was already a tenant at Padam Building when the Kasliwal family moved in there. She watched them come in, bringing boxes and bags along. As a good neighbour should, her parents advised her to visit the newly arrived family and check if they needed help of any kind. Sheets for the bed, a mattress perhaps? She was to offer them the use of their refrigerator, till theirs arrived. Food could quickly sour in the city's humid climate.

It was a festival day; Shivratri to be precise, when Panna rang the bell and made her neighbourly enquiries. To her amazement, the response was that they appreciated her thoughtfulness, but had everything; they had come prepared.

The Kasliwals at Padam were by now a large family. Shankarlal and his third wife and their children had come to Bombay too on Shambhu Kumar's insistence. They occupied a flat of their own, in Padam 1, the building opposite Padam 2, where Shankarlal's sons lived. The three brothers, Abhay Kumar, Shambhu Kumar and Sumati Kumar, together with their wives, occupied the three bedrooms in another flat. The six children would spread mattresses and sleep in the hall. Panna often

A HAPPY HOME | L TO R | AMBUJ, VIKAS, RAJKUMARI, NITIN, MUKUL, SHAMBHUKUMAR

MUKUL, VIKAS, NITIN

VIKAS, MUKUL, SHRIJA

NEERJA & MUKUL

SHRIJA & UMANG

VIKAS & WARIJ

> STRESS CREEPS IN ONLY IF YOU ARE NOT STRONG; IT IS A SIGN OF
> WEAKNESS. AND THE BEST WAY TO AVOID STRESS IS TO ALIGN YOUR
> THOUGHTS, WORDS AND ACTIONS. *MANN MEIN HO SO VACHAN SE
> KAHIYE, VACHAN SE HO VO TANN SE KARIYE.*
>
> – SHAMBHU KUMAR

imagined the pillow fights and whispered giggles that must prelude sleep as the children wound down for the night.

The house ran on a routine that ensured everyone had time and space for the occupations of the day. Panna's father noticed Shambhu Kumar leaving for work with strict adherence to time. He would mention at the dinner table his admiration for his new neighbour who was, 'hardworking, yet took time to play squash, have outings with the children in the evenings and play bridge on Sundays.'

Panna would often listen to the strains of Jain bhajans rising from the Kasliwal home in the mornings. Later in the day, the music would be from Hindi films. She loved hearing the family sing, 'Everyone sings,' she noticed, and she liked listening to Kaki who would hum while cooking. Shambhu Kumar too enjoyed film songs.

Though they did not seem to have a large social circle, the close-knit family and the fact that Shambhu Kumar and his wife continued to enjoy each other's company, they were, in Rajkumari's words, 'a world unto ourselves.'

Shambhu Kumar was a chain smoker for many years, easily working his way from one lit cigarette to another through a tin of Gold Flake. And if by some mischance, there was not enough stock at home, Rajkumari remembers, 'there would be hell'! As he would let lose his famous temper.

Yet he would, by a superhuman exercise of will, give it up in the early '60s, when a doctor advised him to do so, as it was a risk to his heart. He would never pick up a cigarette again, and drop the habit of chewing tobacco too, which he would indulge, while outside the home.

A day of hard work would be set off by the warmth of family life, when the men stepped into the embrace of their home, with good food, and the chatter of children. Anyone watching the extended family could not but notice that none of the elders made any distinction between the children; outsiders would never be able to tell who was whose child. Of her experience in sharing her home with her brothers-in-law and their families, Rajkumari has insights to offer. 'It's not that you would do something special for your children and leave the rest out. It was all a matter of understanding one another, and taking care of each other's kids.' When she had to go to Kashmir with her husband, without her youngest child, daughter Neerja, then only two-and-a-half months old for an entire month, she left her behind with a calm heart, knowing her baby would be fully taken care of in her absence, and not even miss her presence. Not surprising either, was the fact that her niece and nephew, Shrija and Warij, went with them on the trip.

The two older wives, Kamala and Rajkumari, enjoyed each other's company and along with Malti, Sumati Kumar's wife, they would spend hours cooking up a storm in the kitchen. When the husbands came home, the focus would turn on them. Often Panna, living right opposite the Kasliwal home, would catch glimpses of the family eating, and notice that Shambhu Kumar and his wife were eating from the same thali. 'My parents never, ever did that,' she mused.

By this time, the Kasliwal daughters-in-law would add sewing to their list of skills. A tutor was employed for this purpose, and the ladies would bend industriously over the flowers and birds they were being taught to create with the needle. Umang and Shrija, the adolescent daughters of the family, would also participate.

By the end of 1970, a fast growing family forced the Kasliwals to separate their living space; Shambhu Kumar and his family moved into a separate flat in Padam, while Sumati Kumar and family moved to an adjoining building. The kitchen remained common, which, Shankarlal and his family included, totalled 27.

Their home was a warm and open place for friends and family. Always a full-house, with celebrations and get-togethers happening round the year.

Panna enjoyed cooking and realising she was adept at some dishes, the Kasliwal kitchen would be opened to her, with requests that she make some of her finest dishes. 'I would keep it simple as the quantities would be huge, so *dhokla* or something along those lines.' She'd learn that Shambhu Kumar liked a variety of dishes to be served at every meal.

Without fail, before he went to work, every single day, Shambhu Kumar would drop in to meet his elder brother, and repeat the visit on his return before going to his own home.

L TO R | AMBUJ, WARIJ, SHANKARLAL, VIKAS, MANOJ, MUKUL

SHANKARLAL WITH THE FAMILY | PADAM BUILDING

Panna adds that she found a role model in Rajkumari, with whom she forged a special bond. She admired the fact that though she dressed traditionally, wearing a sari in the Gujarati style, with the *pallu* in front, Kaki would be as busy as any modern woman, dashing in and out of the building, driving about in her car … 'she inspired me to learn to drive. I got my licence as soon as I turned 18,' she remembers.

The entire Kasliwal clan was in full attendance at Panna's wedding.

When Panna married and moved to Marine Drive to live with her husband and his joint family, her visits to the Kasliwal home decreased. But whenever she visited her parents, she would drop in and meet the family. And in a very natural way, Panna found herself a part of the Kasliwal family's favourite outings. 'My husband and I became close friends with Kaka-Kaki, and we often would sit at a game of Bridge. Gone were the days when I was scared of Kaka, and would run home when he entered the house in the evenings. We would often go on picnics, and on road trips carrying food, eating from dishes placed on top of the car. At times we carried a folding table and chairs. I love going on *teerth yatras*, and went with them on countless pilgrimages,' she remembers. 'And though they were obviously blessed with a swiftly growing prosperity, and I could see how the number of their cars in the compound was increasing, and how they were buying bigger, better models, nothing about their behaviour changed. Through our travels, they would show the utmost concern for me, and take care of all my needs. And of course, though I would buy my flight tickets, they would never ever let me pay for anything else. I would have to find gifts to give them later, using some occasion as an excuse in an attempt to repay them.' Her most memorable pilgrimage was visiting Bahubali during the *abhishek* that happens once in 12 years.

SHAMBHU KUMAR & RAJKUMARI | SAMMED SHIKHAR JI | JHARKHAND

AT GOMATESHWARA | KARNATAKA

AT SHRINATH JI | NATHDWARA | RAJASTHAN

In fact, the Kasliwal pilgrimages were all-encompassing events, where families and many others would be included, depending on whosoever was free and able to join. Though they were Jains and visited all the famous Jain *teerth sthaans* like Sammed Shikhar ji, Sankeshwar Parshwanath, Mahudi Padamprabhu, Mahavir ji near Jaipur, the pilgrimages also extended to temples in Shirdi, Ujjain, Badrinath, Kedarnath, Tirupati, and were as much occasions for bonding and relaxation as they were for spiritual concentration.

Abhay Kumar and Shambhu Kumar would go on to build a home in the heart of Indore, a sprawling yet warm bungalow named after the darling of the family. Neerja Villa, a world within a world that Rajkumari would manage efficiently. ⑤

A LEADER IS BORN

One of the most eloquent reflections of the success of a leader and his leadership style, is the way his employees look at him, and whether the turnover rate of employed personnel is high or low. Shambhu Kumar can boast of countless employees who have been with the organisation for four or more decades!

Punamchand Daga, Mukesh Fadia, Ashok Shah, among the earliest of people to work with the man they earlier called 'Bhaiya Saheb' and now refer to as 'Kaka Saheb,' have stories to tell of their growth in the company and the reasons for their loyalty to the Group.

Ashok Kumar Goyle joined S.Kumars in 1986, though he had met Shambhu Kumar in Dewas in 1977, where he had been employed as a Sales Manager with Dewas Textiles. 'We had a conversation at that time,' Goyle says. Perhaps, the spark Shambhu Kumar had seen in the young sales manager remained in his memory, and prompted him to insist that Goyle take charge of the S.Kumars' marketing divisions in Dewas and Bombay. 'For personal reasons, I had to stay in Delhi, so I ended up looking after North India,' says Goyle.

Goyle would, in Shambhu Kumar's words, "earn the dubious distinction of interacting with the entire family," as he was roped in to do 'all sorts of work that included coordinating travel and pilgrimages. I would go along too,' he adds, as he recollects the first visit made by Shambhu Kumar's family to Vaishno Devi. 'There was no helicopter ride possible at that time, so we used horses, and that trip was a precursor to many more. I think I accompanied the family five or six times to that very holy shrine alone.'

To begin with, Goyle's work included establishing an office in Delhi in the hub of the textile market, setting up associate dealers and looking after procuring their orders directly from Dewas; as well as billing, payments, and, when necessary, sorting out the problems dealers may face.

Goyle says the agent he took over from in Delhi had worked with S.Kumars for 25 years. He was considered almost a family member, but left as, 'he had become too old. When I took over, I faced a lot of resistance from a number of Bombay people in the Group. However, Kaka Saheb stood staunchly by me,' he adds. 'Those

days we still called him Bhaiya Saheb, he became Kaka Saheb to us only after Dada Saheb, his elder brother's demise.'

Though he retired three years ago, as Vice President, Marketing, Northern Region, after 33 years with the Group, Goyle has vibrant memories of his interactions with Shambhu Kumar. 'He changed my perception of bosses; I have not enjoyed or experienced such love and affection from anyone else in my 40-year-long career. When I requested him to relieve me he said, "You are leaving the company, but not the family."

'Though, he was a hard task master, and would demand targets be met, and expansion of business be a constant. Yet, his business style was so different; he was the first in the textile industry to bond with dealers and associates; and call everybody by their first names. This is what makes dealers work exclusively for S.Kumars. Many competitors have tried to shake their loyalty, but they do not budge an inch,' he says.

'And despite his age, he is still hands-on. In fact, he even countered my request for retirement with, "When I have not retired yet, how can you?"'

SHAMBHU KUMAR & WIFE WELCOME MARTIN HENRY & FAMILY

WITH CLOSE FRIEND & ASSOCIATE D.P. MALOO

IN DISCUSSION | RAIPUR

WITH TEAM | INDORE | 1977

Goyle believes that other companies try, 'but cannot forge the kind of bonds Kaka does with his team,' adding that 'though he was the boss, Kaka would never sit in my chair. "I have enough problems, you handle what the chair brings to you," he would say. I found it a profound thought.

'The charm of working for S.Kumars was unique,' Goyle says nostalgically. 'I worked for myself, it was my investment in self-growth, an immersive experience. That's how we operated! What I have learnt from Kaka, I will carry for the rest of my life.'

Ashok Shah had a matriculate certificate from a Gujarati medium school to his name, when he joined in 1965. He was following up on a suggestion that he try for employment with S.Kumars. Though he knew no English

and much of the paperwork was in English, he showed his eagerness to learn and was taken on. 'There was no appointment letter, I was just told to join as a semi-clerk, and started work.' His duties included 'this and that,' odd jobs that required doing. Soon enough he learnt to write bills. After a two-year stint as a telephone operator, he was taken as Sales Assistant to Shambhu Kumar's younger brother, Sumati Kumar who had joined S.Kumars in Marketing and Sales of whom Shambhu Kumar said to the MD of Madura Mills, 'If you sit long enough, he will sell you too!' Shah sold cloth produced by Laxmi Vishnu Mills and Madura Mills, and would later sell the cloth his bosses' mills produced, working with the next generation, and then directly with 'Kaka Saheb.'

Right through, he declares, he was trained as a son would be, and in due course could take over sales for all of Bombay, moving on to the all-important West Zone, including Goa, Gujarat and parts of Madhya Pradesh.

'People would come to buy, we never had to canvass, such was our relationship with dealers. I would ask them their requirement and coordinate for timely supply. Our dealings were on the lines shown to us by Kaka Saheb; which is why we have dealers or associates as we prefer to call them, who have been with us over the past 50 to 60 years, through second or even third generations now.'

Om Prakash Pacheria is 80 years old now, but looks back with fondness on his time with the S.Kumars Group; an association that spans 57 years and counting. He was working with Kohinoor Mills in 1965, where the material Shambhu Kumar had bought for suitings, would come for processing. There were only three mills in the country that could boast of being able to use 130 degrees C temperature and the high pressure that the dyeing process required; Kohinoor Mills was one of the three. Dyeing of polyester was not possible without these machines. Pacheria remembers he, 'came in contact with Kaka at that time when he was still a trader, buying cloth, processing it and selling.'

Pacheria gives a valuable insight into the technical aspects and Shambhu Kumar's approach to the limitations of the process. Once the material came to us, he said, 'The greige fabric would be cleaned, dried and heat set at 200 degrees C for the polyester fibre. There was a special machine "Zero-Zero," to stabilise the fabric and make it shrink proof.

'However, if 100 metres of cloth would be fed into the machine, we could get 96 metres as output. The machine was set to 2-4 per cent shrinkage.'

After the heat set process, the fabric would go through the high temperature, high pressure dyeing machines. These earlier machines had a more involved process

> # THERE ARE SOME PEOPLE WHO ARE BORN GREAT, SOME WHO BECOME GREAT AND SOME WHO HAVE GREATNESS THRUST ON THEM ... *RAM SE BADA RAM KA NAAM* ... LET OTHERS THINK OF YOU AS BIG.
>
> – SHAMBHU KUMAR

with open fabrics. The newer jet dyeing technique included fabrics being dyed in rope form.

Only the polyester would be dyed, the fabric needed to run on another machine to colour the viscose. 'Shades of both had to be manually matched perfectly, and I had been trained by the German technicians on how to do this and run the machines.'

Pacheria would move on to work directly with S.Kumars when their first processing unit, SKM Fabrics, was set up in Andheri. And be one of the key players in setting up the factory in Dewas. Though he retired from an active role, he continues with the Group companies in a consulting capacity. But more of that later.

When Punamchand Daga joined the Vithalwadi office in 1967 with responsibilities in both, maintaining accounts and helping in marketing, he remembers that weavers would come to the office to sell cloth. He would oversee the buying of shirting material; and extend his role to keep an eye on what was selling well, and advise accordingly. 'Co-ordinates for schools were the most popular,' he remembers, adding, 'I would report to Kaka at a meeting held between 10 and 12, every day. Kaka kept his finger on the pulse of the market; nothing escaped him, and he was very particular that everything should be done properly, honestly and in time. Any other way would make him very angry. But he was genuinely caring about all of us. Never treated us differently

from his sons, and demanded the same discipline and attitude towards work from them too.' Daga has, in turn, worked with Abhay Kumar's older son, Ambuj, and also Vikas and Nitin, Shambhu Kumar's sons. He credits Shambhu Kumar's approach to work and people for the unparalleled success of the company.

Mukesh Fadia shares the belief that Shambhu Kumar built a company where anyone could grow to his full capacity. He was 18 years old, and had completed his 12th class, when he joined S.Kumars in 1972; his job was to take sales delivery from the godown. His conviction comes from the fact that despite the lack of a formal degree in accounting, the company's CA handed some accounting work to him,

IF YOU DO NOT GROW EVERY YEAR THEN YOU ARE NOT IN THE RIGHT PLACE. KEEP UP WITH THE MARKET ... WE NEVER TRIED TO COMPETE, BUT WHEN OTHERS SAW US AS COMPETITORS WE FELT GOOD.

– SHAMBHU KUMAR

as he had time on hand. 'I learnt steadily under his guidance and by 1976, had joined the accounts department full-time.'

Fadia had an occasion to get a taste of 'Kaka's' famous temper. He smiles at the memory of what might have been a shocking event at the time it occurred.

By 2002, Fadia was well acquainted with the company's policies, its ways of working. He felt he was indeed a member of the extended family. 'I had been given some account books to update, and was working on them,' he recollects, 'it was slow and painstaking work, it took all of four months for me to clear. Always wanting to get things done meticulously and on time, Kaka, upset over how long it had taken, called me and told me I was fired. He felt I was slow and lax at completing the task on hand. I was shaken. But when he understood how time consuming it was for me to ensure each and every old entry in the numerous ledgers was correct, and reconcile every entry, he changed his decision at once. He admitted that he had not realised, and insisted I should stay and continue. I was a small person, he did not have to admit he had misjudged the situation; but his anger disappeared as quickly as it had flared.' Fadia still heads accounts, and the relationship with Shambhu Kumar has endured. 'I could not believe it when I learnt that Kaka and Kaki were coming to attend my daughter's wedding,' he says.

Attending the weddings of the children of their employees, ensuring medical aid in dire cases; Shambhu Kumar's mantra

for nurturing long-term relationships with his people went a long way in strengthening the Group, holding it strong against competition.

Not just employees, but agents and dealers too are extended the same courtesies, and allowed to grow. 'It's a relationship built on mutual trust,' as Prakash Ranka puts it. Ranka joined his father in 1976, who had been a selling agent for the South since 1962. Their agency coordinates between the mills and the dealers, and works with the principal group, S.Kumars. As an agent, Ranka explains, the liability of payment rests with him. He appoints dealers who do the selling.

When he started in 1976, Ranka and his father looked after Karnataka and Kerala. Their main competition was from Binny's, Davangere Cotton Mills and Mafatlal. By 1981, Coimbatore was added to their list, and then, like a conquering emperor annexing territories, the duo had the entire South India, inclusive of all of Tamil Nadu and Andhra Pradesh as their jurisdiction. He now has offices in Hyderabad, Chennai, Coimbatore and Bengaluru, and were it not for Covid, 'we would have hit our target of doubling our turnover.'

Through the years with S.Kumars, Ranka says he has learnt a lot, about human relations. 'Kaka Saheb makes no difference between big and small dealers, he does not discriminate ... in trade conferences, or when a dealer visits Mumbai, he is treated very well, with love and courtesy.' Whenever any dealer visits Mumbai, one sure-shot stop is the

S.Kumars office in Niranjan Building at Marine Drive, which has been a constant since the '70s.

Ranka shares some more of the formulae that make Shambhu Kumar's enterprises succeed. 'Kaka Saheb has always insisted on offering the highest quality at the lowest price. He knows every aspect of production perfectly and ensures his mills have a fast rotation of material; achieving a 33-day process of yarn-to-finished fabric, instead of the usual 90 days.

'He floats incentive schemes for dealers, and ensures they get the promised prizes. And when at the dealer conferences, new products that are being launched are introduced to the dealers, they are wrapped in motivating schemes. It is business plus fun at every conference. And if there are problems, either between the company and the dealer, or something the dealer is facing in the marketplace, there is a move to resolve it quickly through positive talks.

'Nitin, Vikas, Ambuj ... we are like family. They visit us whenever they are in Bengaluru.' Like Panna Javeri, Ranka also has fond memories of being invited on the *teerth yatra* to witness the *Maha-mastak-abhishek* of Gomateshwar at Shravanabelagola. 'Though my brother handles other mills, I have stayed mainly with S.Kumars,' he says. When his father started working for Reliance, Ranka adds, 'Kaka Saheb once asked him what the difference was between Reliance and S.Kumars. My father told him, "Reliance is a hotel; S.Kumars is home." ⊛

A RAGS TO RICHES STORY

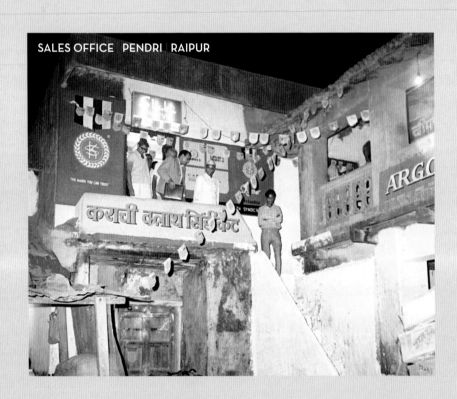

SALES OFFICE PENDRI | RAIPUR

MEETING WITH TRADERS | RAIPUR

Pannalal Dave bore it for six months before he decided to speak up. He had a huge cache of fent rags and though he managed to sell them easily enough, it was not giving him any worthwhile return. The money was not enough to keep the home fires burning.

Pannalal had started assisting his father when he turned 18. His father had two partners in a dealership that sourced goods from S.Kumars and everything had been going well enough, till a disagreement arose between the three partners. As the dispute seemed irreconcilable, the partnership was dissolved. The Daves started on their own, with the father and two sons, Pannalal and his brother. Till then, the company had been dealing in fent rags and saris. Now, a division needed to be made so there would be no conflict between the groups who had separated. 'We drew chits to divide the goods,' Pannalal says, 'the other partners got the saris, we got the fent rags, which were sold by weight.' It was less prestigious than saris, but that was the luck of the draw and the Daves had no option but to go with it. They would try and sell the polyester cut pieces and fent rags and hope to make it work.

But as Pannalal soon discovered, eking a profit from his share of goods seemed impossible. After trying his best for six months, he made bold to approach

Shambhu Kumar and explained his difficulty to him; the price of 95 rupees was not viable at all. 'Kaka Saheb listened to what I had to say,' Pannalal says. 'He was impressed that I had tried to make it work for six whole months, before placing my problem to him. And he immediately found a solution. He cut the price of my goods from 95 to 70 rupees. Making it easy for me to sell at a decent profit.'

Once the relationship was established, the young dealer found things moving smoothly. Other opportunities would rise, and he would be quick to use his ingenuity to make the most of them. Pannalal shares another story:

'About 250 bales of Teresilk were lying in S.Kumars Mills, with no one willing to pick them. Woven as ladies' suitings, the width was only 48 inches. I asked to pick a small portion of it, and sold the lot width-wise, as pant pieces. In three months, the entire lot was picked up.'

When at Diwali time the loft at the Vithalwadi office groaned under the weight of defective or returned pieces, Shambhu Kumar, realising that Pannalal had the gift of salesmanship, told his staff to sell the full stock to him at one rupee a metre. 'I cut it, and sold it all at a neat profit,' Pannalal says brightly. It was enough of an achievement to make the 21-year-old feel overjoyed.

Pannalal found he had Shambhu Kumar's blessing to set him on his way. Business grew by 50 per cent a year. 'Kaka Saheb would even give fresh stock at a lower rate after getting the seconds stamp marked on it, and this was only to support me,' he says. 'Kaka would watch quietly, without my knowledge, keep an eye on the goods I was buying, and what varieties I chose. One year, when my turnover fell from five crores to three crores, he set it right.'

The Dave brothers, in turn, proved their loyalty to Shambhu Kumar. 'For 20 years we were number one, we bought most of the fent rags and cut pieces from S.Kumars.'

Though he attended the dealer meetings, Pannalal kept his counsel, and would continue to buy directly from the principal, rather than through an agent. 'For one, I was not booking fresh *maal*. And Kaka Saheb trusted me, knew I would never default,' he says.

These days, his son handles the business. 'He only buys fresh stock, no seconds,' the proud father says. 'And only from S.Kumars, no other mills. Not till date.'

Of such simple stories about trust and support are great businesses built. ⑤

SIX YARDS OF FAME

The 1970s were perhaps the most significant years in the trajectory of S.Kumars as a leading textile company. The decade when the name would become synonymous with cloth, not just in the cities and principal towns of the country, but filter through to smaller districts and tehsils in the hinterlands. In its third decade, S.Kumars would zero in on its selling mantra.

This is particularly significant considering that, in the background, the nation was going through a series of turbulent events … some good, others likely to shatter the country as it had been envisioned by the Constitution.

Among the milestones were the frontiers, the nation, just stepping into its thirties, was pushing. Matching the promise of the Green Revolution that would lead India to self-sufficiency in wheat and food grain; a milk revolution, Operation Flood, is launched by the National Dairy Development Board with an aim to make India the world's top producer of milk. Indira Gandhi stages a comeback with the Indian National Congress (I), a party she has formed, after she was expelled from Congress {O} for breaking party discipline, and wins a landslide victory. Project Tiger is launched to conserve the animal's habitats and prevent its extinction; Aryabhatta, India's first space shuttle is launched and starts to gaily scan the firmament. India's first nuclear explosion at Pokhran would follow

in a few years. A retaliatory war against Pakistan wins East Pakistan independence, with India playing a lead role in the birth of Bangladesh. Sanjay Gandhi starts an initiative to build the country's first small car, a car the middle class can afford. A little known wannabe actor, Amitabh Bachchan, stakes his claim to stardom by donning the mantle of 'angry young man,' an antithesis of the romantic hero that had wooed audiences through the '60s.

On the flip side, Sanjay Gandhi's forced sterilisation programme sends shock waves across the country. And when Emergency is declared by Indira Gandhi, the country is shocked and divided into those who suffer it silently and disbelievingly, and those who work towards a retaliation. Retribution does indeed follow; the country shakes off the Emergency at the elections, and for the first time since Independence, the Opposition, in the colours of the Janata Party, comes into power. Democracy had flexed its muscles and the voice of the people had spoken against oppression of any kind.

Laxman Vaman Apte was going through his own upheavals too. After 65 years or more of his family successfully running Kohinoor Mills, it seemed as if he would need to look elsewhere to continue his business. When a big player in the share market, Chunilal 'Tiger' Kapadia took over the shares of Kantilal Nahalchand, one of Apte's partners, Apte felt that he did not wish

to continue with Kohinoor Mills. The third partner, Mafatlal Gangalbhai, was of the same opinion. Selling their shares to Kapadia, the two partners washed their hands of Kohinoor Mills, exiting with grace and ending an association of generations and decades.

Though they had already acquired Kamal Dyeing and Swastik Dyeing in Bombay, Apte was still looking out for another mill to continue his manufacturing business. He found a likely purchase in Lakshmi Vishnu Mills, located in Solapur. The Vissanji family, major shareholders in the mill, were looking for a suitable buyer. When approached, they offered 'controlling interest' in the plant. By the last quarter of 1969, he had acquired charge of the management. Lakshmi and Vishnu, though bracketed as one name, were actually two separate mills that had only been amalgamated a few years before Apte acquired controlling shares. Apte changed the spelling of Lakshmi to Laxmi and set about making the mills spin gold for him, as Kohinoor had done.

An intriguing anecdote deserves retelling. Lakshmi Mills, which dated back to 1898, was started by a cotton trader, Lakhamsi. A famine was raging at that time, and workers worked for *chane phutane*, in lieu of cash. This would get the mill the nickname *phutanechi girni*. Lakhamsi ran out of money. He sold the mills to a British trading house that completed the factory and got it running.

Stroll in your Garden,
wherever you go.
Win First Prize
at your own Flower Show.

Buds, blossoms, blooms...petal-soft sarees spun
from sheer 'Terene' — the fabric that needs no
tending. Fabulous 'Terene' drapes like a
clinging vine...stays dew-drop fresh, that.
From Laxmi Vishnu's flower-beds of fashion fabrics
and their saree-scape artist, Dinoo Vacha.

"Own one of my Originals"
says Laxmi Vishnu's Dinoo.
"They're expensive of course.
But then, for you Flower Child,
money grows on trees."

LAXMI VISHNU NEW 100% 'Terene' Sarees

S. Kumar merchandise

Hello Discotheque Dolly,
where have you been?
Swinging and swirling
in teeny 'Terene'

We've got Carnaby Colours to light up your scene.
In unflappable, zappable, turned on 'Terene'.
Water just drops out. As for ironing, you can
cop out.
Woven real wild by Laxmi Vishnu.
And Dinoo psychedelicately designed 'em.
Crazy.

"Own one of my Originals"
says Laxmi Vishnu's Dinoo.
"They're expensive of course.
So get lucky, little girl."

LAXMI VISHNU NEW 100% 'Terene' Sarees

S. Kumar merchandise

TERENE SARIS LAUNCHED WITH STRIKING AD CAMPAIGN IN THE TIMES OF INDIA | SEPTEMBER 1970

Icicle pastels, soft serene
A crisp morning saree
of pure 'Terene'

Rise and shine. Be a morning sprite, all carefree
and bright in the dew-kissed colours of a gossamer-
light saree—made from 100% pure 'Terene'.

Lavishly woven by Laxmi Vishnu.
'Good Morning' designs by Dinoo Vacha.

"Own one of my Originals"
says Laxmi Vishnu's Dinoo.
"They're expensive of course.
Everything exclusive is."

LAXMI VISHNU NEW 100% 'Terene' Sarees

S. Kumar merchandise

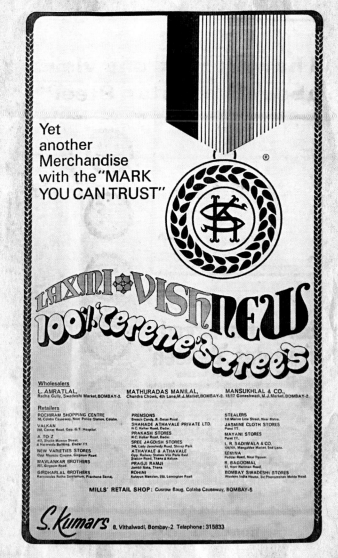

Yet
another
Merchandise
with the "MARK
YOU CAN TRUST"

LAXMI VISHNU NEW 100% 'Terene' Sarees

Wholesalers

L. AMRATLAL,
Radha Gully, Swadeshi Market, BOMBAY-2.

MATHURADAS MANILAL,
Chandra Chowk, 4th Lane, M.J.Market, BOMBAY-2.

MANSUKHLAL & CO.,
15/17 Ganeshwadi, M.J.Market, BOMBAY-2.

Retailers

ROCHIRAM SHOPPING CENTRE
30, Colaba Causeway, Near Police Station, Colaba.

VALKAN
308, Carnac Road, Opp. G.T. Hospital.

A TO Z
410, Shaikh Memon Street,
& Harawala Building, Dadar T.T.

NEW VARIETIES STORES
Opp. Majestic Cinema, Girgaum Road.

MAVLANKAR BROTHERS
387, Girgaum Road.

GIRDHARLAL BROTHERS
Karmondas Natha Sanitorium, Prarthana Samaj.

PREMSONS
Breach Candy, B. Desai Road.

SHAHADE ATHAVALE PRIVATE LTD.
N.C. Kelkar Road, Dadar.

PRAKASH STORES
N.C. Kelkar Road, Dadar.

SREE JAGDISH STORES
248, Lady Jamshedji Road, Shivaji Park.

ATHAVALE & ATHAVALE
Opp. Railway Station Vile Parle East.

PRAGJI RAMJI
Jambli Naka, Thana.

ROHINI
Natraya Mansion, 230, Lamington Road.

STEALERS
1st Marine Line Street, Near Metro.

JASMINE CLOTH STORES
Plot TT.

MAYANI STORES
Parel TT.

L. R. SADIWALA & CO.
126/101, Mangaldas Market, 2nd Lane.

EEMINA
Poddar Road, Near Tijewer.

R. BAGOOMAL
91, Vyer Naliman Road.

BOMBAY SWADESHI STORES
Western India House, Sir Pherozeshah Mehta Road.

MILLS' RETAIL SHOP: Cusrow Baug, Colaba Causeway, BOMBAY-5.

S. Kumars 8, Vithalwadi, Bombay-2. Telephone: 315833

AT ANNUAL MEETING

BHAU SAHEB WITH ABHAY KUMAR, SHAMBHU KUMAR & SONS

Bhau Saheb Apte, with the help of his son, Madhav, who had joined the business, set about modernising the mills and its output. He had to change its image. Seen as a second class country mill, it was not in sync with his lifestyle or vision. By calling in the dealers of Kohinoor Mills, he sold the huge inventory of unsold cloth, ranging from superfine cottons to greige cloth, and started introducing innovative material to his looms. Soon enough, the mills were creating fine cotton cloth varieties like 2x2 voiles and poplins, which he had been rolling out in Kohinoor Mills. Polyester suitings and shirtings came next. The dealers who had worked with V.S. Apte and Sons followed, eager to pick up the materials. Turnover, according to Shambhu Kumar's recollections, would have been '100s of crores.'

It was at this point in the history of Laxmi Vishnu Mills that Shambhu Kumar would end up playing a key role. When Apte wanted to push the production of synthetic cloth higher, it helped that he had, thanks to Shambhu Kumar, almost a monopoly arrangement with CAFI.

To Shambhu Kumar goes too the credit for the huge success of the 'Terene' sari. Cotton and silk were the materials saris were woven of at that time. Silk was expensive and thus for special occasions. Cotton was best suited for daily wear and the weather conditions for most part of the year, and designs and weaves differed from state to state and region to region, offering a huge variety to choose from. Yet, cotton crumpled with wear, and with more women entering the workplace, ironing the wrinkles out became a necessary chore. Besides, cotton took a long while to dry in the monsoon. A sari made of synthetic material might eliminate these shortcomings and find favour.

Nylon, a filament which was in vogue at that time, in the mid '60s, had a significant drawback in the fact that the material, like its co-product, plastic, could not let air pass through, and so did not allow the skin to breathe. In a humid and hot climate like India, nylon was almost unwearable as a garment.

Shambhu Kumar, who had studied all aspects of cloth production by then, having spent every free minute in various departments of Kohinoor Mills, watching, asking questions and learning, came up with a suggestion. Soon, the R&D of Laxmi Vishnu Mills would be experimenting with blending viscose fibre with the polyester fibre at the spinning stage. The high tech machines would then print the material as required. Once printed, the material would go through a carbonisation process, and the acid would eat through the viscose, leaving behind polyester fabric. Soft and pliable, and more important, easy on the skin.

The new machines of the mill that Apte had inherited printed brightly coloured designs and patterns on the fabric. This in turn, led to a new idea from Ramesh

THE S.KUMARS TEAM DEALER CONFERENCE

WHEN I SOWED A SEED, I DID NOT KNOW! THAT SEED ONE DAY WOULD GROW, INTO A HUGE PROSPEROUS ADMIRABLE TREE, AND GIVE ME SHELTER.

– BHAU SAHEB APTE

Singhal of CAFI: to print saris of terylene, branded as 'Terene.'

A design department was already in place, to create the enticing prints for the material. Apte now recruited Dinoo Dossabhoy to create printed fantasies on six-yard lengths that the mills would send out as saris. Both Shambhu Kumar and Apte were sure that the easy-to-maintain, attractive saris would find instant appeal. The saris were indeed soft and silky. The claim was they could go through a finger ring, perhaps 'inspired' by the story of Dacca muslin that was woven for Akbar's daughter, yards of which could indeed go through a ring.

Excise duty made a huge impact on pricing, but Shambhu Kumar kept the mass market in mind. And decided to keep the price low. To achieve maximum sales. Hence, the price point was 99 rupees.

To further push their new product in the market, Dossabhoy suggested they hold fashion shows. Little did she know that this one idea of hers would go on to create raves.

They were right. The saris spun by Laxmi Vishnu Mills were quickly picked up by women captivated by the fabric and prints. The saris, though woven by Apte's Mill, came to be known in the market as 'S.Kumar ki Sariyan,' as

S.Kumars was the sole selling agent for the saris. Khatau and Garden Silk Mills would also step into the synthetic sari space shortly after, but once again, Shambhu Kumar had ensured his mentor had first mover advantage.

As Ashok Shah, Vice President, Marketing, Western Region, says, 'We had dealers for the saris across India. Laxmi Vishnu Mills were producing 10 lakh metres of saris every month, carrying the S.Kumars brand name.'

'Terene' saris raged as a must-have for a long period. When the fashion winds changed direction. And the fire of 'Terene' saris burnt low, the production was stopped. ◉

RAMPING THINGS UP

S.Kumars moved into the stratosphere of success, when Shambhu Kumar met Shambhu Kumar. 'We share a first name, but Shambhu Kumar was one of the most fiercely competitive men I have met,' said Shambhu Sista, popularly known as Bobby Sista, of Sista's Sales and Publicity Services. 'He somehow knew just how to do things just right. Shambhu Kumar was the superlative ad man, it was in his blood. For example, he ensured that every bolt of cloth that left S.Kumars carried a small card inside which read something to the effect of, "We are S.Kumars, and are in textiles, in synthetics, contributing to promoting blends," and it helped immensely to create awareness about the company.'

The two men met courtesy Madhav Apte, as Bobby's agency was already handling the Laxmi Vishnu Mills account.

Shambhu Kumar gave his namesake a simple brief: he wanted to popularise synthetics, as a more viable substitute for the more expensive cotton fabric, and extend their distribution across India, including in the small towns and villages.

'That's how the fashion shows started,' Sista says, 'as a means to getting the maximum number of retailers into the fold.' It was a novel idea, and it would take off like a wild fire.

Rupa Sangle, who worked at Sista's, says Abhay Kumar shared the honours for the marketing ideas that pushed S.Kumars into becoming a national brand. 'They believed in backward integration,' she says, of the brothers' way of working. Abhay Kumar, she adds, believed that it was the man behind the counter who was more important than the man who reads your ad. Thus, 'the dealer was the vital link; if the man behind the counter believed in the goods, he would do his best to sell it. And so, the focus was on the dealers. And trade-meets would be held all over India.'

The masterstroke of S.Kumars was they created a Retailer Gift Unit scheme, according to the value of the goods. And incentives were built into the scheme, both at the buying and the selling stage … so retailers would be motivated to pick more goods from dealers, as well as sell more. They would go on to collect a huge database of over 35,000 retailers from all across the country through this scheme.

When the fashion shows were launched as a way to familiarise dealers about the products on offer, audio-visual ads were part of the package. Sangle, proficient in Hindi, created the first ever Hindi jingle for S.Kumars. 'Jingles in Hindi became very popular later,' she explains, 'but as I was a Hindi copywriter, I instinctively came up with a jingle in Hindi, and it clicked.' Partly because Abhay Kumar preferred Hindi, and the dealers also found it easier to understand the message. 'They were not just glamour events,' Sangle says. 'They were trade shows. And everything was done in Hindi.'

The product was male oriented, as the thrust was on suitings, and the focus was on suit lengths. Male models would walk the ramp, and a commentary in Hindi would give details of the special qualities of the fabric. Sangle remembers how the models, mostly English medium educated, would react saying they could not relate to the Hindi commentary. 'I would tell them there was no need to react, they just had to walk the ramp.'

'The fashion shows built the S.Kumars brand, but built my mother's career too,' says Sangeeta Chopra, who owns an art gallery, Art Musings in Colaba, in South Mumbai. And indeed, when Sangeeta's mother, Shanti Chopra, who had been working with Femina magazine to orchestrate their fashion shows, left to launch her own company, it was S.Kumars

ABHAY KUMAR | MARKETING MEET

SHAMBHU KUMAR & FAMILY WITH MODELS | AFTER FASHION SHOW

who gave her the first big break. 'We were handed the project of holding 40 shows in 30 days, all over India; it was a huge breakthrough,' Chopra remembers.

Bobby Sista recollects how the first few fashion shows were held primarily in Bombay, with Shanti Chopra bringing in lovely, sophisticated models. The potential of the shows, he says, caught the attention of Shambhu Kumar, who immediately saw them as a means to take his mission forward. He decided to extend the shows to towns across India, big or small.

Thinking very differently from what a lesser marketing man would have done, Shambhu Kumar decided to place his shows in the most opulent ballrooms of five-star hotels. 'Retailers and dealers will hold us in awe,' he told Sista, 'we will earn their respect.'

It was completely a B-to-B initiative, aimed at the dealer, fuelling his understanding of the goods, and adding to his need to invest in buying and selling it. Instead of costly advertising through mass media,

the company worked by marketing their message to dealers in every town across the country. The idea bore rich fruit as dealers, 'thronged to the events.'

According to Sangle, the fashion shows were thought through for maximum information and impact. Audio-visuals that centred around festivals but highlighting the USPs of the fabrics would be created and beamed to the dealers on the ramp, followed by models wearing garments made of the fabrics. The range of suitings would also be on display, so dealers could actually touch and feel the fabric and understand it for themselves. 'Bhaiya Saheb and Dada Saheb believed in the economy of scale, that selling cheaper would result in higher profit, both to the dealer

and to S.Kumars. Naturally, bookings were immediate.'

If the fashion shows were a thundering success with the audience they were aimed at, it was also because Shanti Chopra and her team worked to set a benchmark. Though she was still in her teens, Sangeeta, Shanti's daughter, was a keen team member. 'We would go to the factory and pick up the fabrics; design the clothes, get them stitched. We would discuss concepts with the Kasliwal brothers and plan the schedules.'

Though they often travelled with the shows, accompanied by top models, both male and female, the Chopras also found ways to make the shows run on remote control. 'Shanti Chopra had designed and given us a portable stage, complete with props. She would send detailed instructions for setting up the show, and we would manage it in the smaller towns,' Sista remembers. 'But

LIVE BAND | DEALER MEET

FASHION SHOW | CRYSTAL ROOM | TAJ MAHAL PALACE HOTEL | BOMBAY

she roped in the best models, from Anna Bredemeyer and Shobha Rajadhyaksha (now De), to Lascelles and Dalip Tahil.' The ratio was four male models and eight female models. 'Kalpana Iyer, Juhi Chawla, Kiran Vairale, Kimi Katkar ... you name the model and she has been part of an S.Kumars show,' Chopra adds.

'They were what we called the "Tamasha shows,"' Sangeeta remembers. 'We projected product ranges and collections for different occasions. Uniforms for defence outfits were always a big hit. Segments of the shows were pure fun; entertainment as soft selling. We would use popular Hindi songs and dances, and break the monotony of the ramp walks. The show would start with casuals, and move to evening wear. We had seven sections; and they included glamorising suitings and dressing the younger set. In one show, all the Kasliwal grandchildren were pressed into service to model school uniforms.'

Sangle gives other details that helped make the shows a talking point in the S.Kumars saga. She believes the strength lay in the simplicity of the communication at the shows as they were aimed at the middle class market.

'They did not believe in videos but preferred audio-visuals,' she says, ' as these could

एस. कुमार्स की शर्टींग सूटींग शान बढ़ाए
एस. कुमार्स के फ़ैब्रिक्स दिन भर साथ निभाए
मज़बूत टिकाऊ और स्मार्ट यूनीफ़ोर्म
संजो लाए हैं एस. कुमार्स

be blown up, and made into posters, and ads as well. Also, there were portions that were marked as changeable, to suit an occasion or a location. If a range had proved popular in a city or town they would show more of that range, and the AV would be modified accordingly.' She was given a free hand to work on the content, but adds that one diktat was never to use drinking glasses in the visuals, in ads or films … thanks to their possible link to alcohol. Even as prizes for dealers, glasses were banned.

In some ways, the Chopra shows for S.Kumars laid the template for the fashion shows that came later. And as time progressed and the company acquired other brands like Reid & Taylor, the shows too evolved to keep in sync with the brands. Sangeeta says a highlight in the show trajectory was the one they put up for Reid & Taylor at the Turf Club in Bombay, where dealers watched in wonder as in a show titled 'Masterstroke,' M.F. Husain painted live and Zakir Hussain played the tabla as models made two entries each … first a walk-through through the trees, and the second, a ramp walk, which ended with them on stage, till one by one, all 24 models were in line for the finale.

Shambhu Kumar and Abhay Kumar and their wives always travelled with the shows. So did the children, at times. Sangeeta, who was of the same age, would find friends among the boys, Ambuj, Warij and all. She remembers how Neerja would sit backstage with her knees drawn up and her chin resting in her hands, and watch wide-eyed as the models donned their costumes and make-up; then quickly take her seat in the front row to watch the show with the rest of the spectators.

All in all, it was a great experience for everyone. The Chopras credit it to Shambhu Kumar and his brother. 'We did thousands of shows for others, after the S.Kumars shows, but these were very different,' Shanti says. 'Because we travelled all over the country, to small places like Ernakulum, Nagpur and Bhilai, which we may have otherwise never visited. The routine could be exacting, sometimes we did two or three shows back to back in a day at some locations, but the way we were treated made it all worthwhile and not at all taxing. We travelled by train, we would get in at night and go straight into rehearsal, but we never said no because of the warmth they showed towards us all. There was never-ending *khana* for everybody, even the technical staff was treated with the same respect and concern. Shambhu Kumar would not eat till every one of the team had eaten. We would get rest days after two hectic show days, a bus would be arranged for us to go sightseeing. Also, we stayed at the best hotels, the Rambagh Palace in Jaipur for example, besides other five star properties.'

Models would later tell Shanti Chopra when working with her on shows for other clients, that S.Kumars had spoilt them. They expected the same treatment from everyone, though it was not always forthcoming.

SANGEETA
BIJLANI

'And most important,' Chopra adds, 'the brothers respected our opinion. They let us do what we knew best, put their faith in us as they did in everyone else.' ⊚

ORDER! ORDER!

When the court bailiff announced the star's name and said 'Haazir Ho' in a voice, loud and clear, the entire nation would sit up and take notice. For the next 30 minutes, it was as if everyone was holding their breath, as the mock inquisition unfurled on radio. The programme … 'S.Kumar ka Filmi Mukkadama.'

'We were involved in the idea of using radio right from the beginning,' Bobby Sista says. 'Shambhu Kumar understood the importance of the medium; he knew it reached homes across the country. We discussed possibilities and "Filmi Mukkadama" was conceived.'

But even before the show that would make S.Kumars a household name, and carry its brand recognition into the smallest towns, the company had been exploring the power of radio.

The first show was called 'Aap aur Hum.' A chatty slot that would span subjects that were free ranging. Anything from talking about festivals to dramatising a story. After India's historic victory at the Cricket World Cup, an entire new range of 'Polyacron' suitings, modelled by Kapil Dev, the cricket captain, was named 'Aap aur Hum' to link in to the programme, which was aimed at the middle class.

Meanwhile Sista was thinking of a programme that might find big takers.

एस.कुमार्स फ़िल्मी मुकदमा

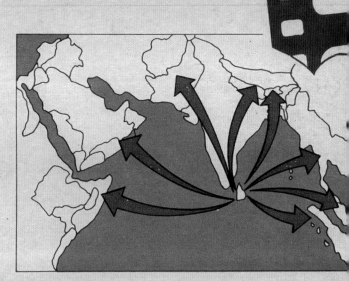

गतवर्ष, १९ अक्तूबर से हर सप्ताह रविवार १०.३० बजे सुबह रेडियो श्रीलंका से यह कार्यक्रम प्रसारित किया जा रहा है। इस कार्यक्रम का मुख्य उद्देश्य हमारे निर्यात-मार्केट के श्रोताओं का मनोरंजन एवं दिलचस्प ढंग से एस.कुमार्स का संदेश उन तक पहुंचाना था, इसीलिये हमने रेडियो श्रीलंका के माध्यम को चुना। पाकिस्तान, बर्मा, मलेशिया, सिंगापुर, हांगकांग, मध्य एशियाई देश, मिस्र, मरीशियस, फीजी, अन्य अफ्रीकी देश तथा नेपाल, भूटान में तो रेडियो श्रीलंका की वाणी गूंज ही रही है, पर बहुत शीघ्र उनके नये ट्रांसमीटर द्वारा हम मध्य योरूप और इंगलैंड तक भी अपना संदेश पहुंचा सकेंगे। यह कार्यक्रम लगातार लोकप्रियता के शिखर पर बढ़ रहा है।

कई मशहूर फिल्मी हस्तियों ने एस.कुमार्स के फिल्मी मुकदमें में, जनता के आरोपों का स्वयं सामना किया। फिल्मी हस्तियों के इन्टरव्यू तो बहुत हुये हैं, पर उन्हें जनता के कटहरे में खड़ा करने का श्रेय, केवल एस.कुमार्स को ही प्राप्त है। एस.कुमार्स की इस अनोखी कचहरी में फिल्मी हस्तियों के जवाब और जनता के वकील, सुप्रसिद्ध अमीन सयानी के दिलचस्प तर्क-वितर्क यानी सोने पे सुहागा।

एस.कुमार्स अपने फिल्मी मुकदमे में हर तीन महीने बाद एक पहेली कार्यक्रम पेश करके, श्रोताओं के मनोरंजन के साथ, उनके लिये उपहार जीतने का स्वर्ण अवसर प्रदान करते हैं। हमारा पहला पहेली-कार्यक्रम २२ फरवरी १९७६ को प्रसारित होने वाला है।

आपको यह जान कर आश्चर्य होगा कि श्रोताओं के अतिरिक्त हमें भारत के ... से भी पत्र आ रहे हैं।

Ameen Sayani: The 'Public Prosecutor'
अमीन सयानी: जनता के वकील—अनोखी इनकी हर दलील

श्रोताओं के पत्र

"आपके कार्यक्रम के बारे में कुछ लिखना सूरजको दिया दिखाने के समान है।" —तरलकुमार, धनबाद

"आपके कार्यक्रम 'फिल्मी मुकदमे' के लिये बहुत शुक्रिया। हम महसूस करते हैं कि एक दिन आपका यह कार्यक्रम सबसे श्रेष्ठ कहलायेगा।" —अबानी कान्ता, उड़ीसा

"आपका मुकदमा सुनने के लिये मेरे घर २५-३० सदस्य इकठ्ठे होते हैं उन्हें प्रोग्राम के साथ साथ चाय भी पिलानी पड़ती है। मेरा आप पर आरोप है कि इतना अच्छा कार्यक्रम पेश करके आप मेरा खर्चा करवाते हैं।" — विरेन्द्र कलसी, भटिंडा

श्रोता अपने प्रिय फिल्मी सितारों, दिलीप कुमार, देव आनन्द, राजेश खन्ना, संजीव कुमार, धर्मेन्द्र, हेमामालिनी, जया, रेखा, ऋषि कपूर, सुनील दत्त, आशा पारेख, हेलन, शशिकपूर, जॉनी वॉकर, जैसी बहुत सी जानी मानी हस्तियों को एस.कुमार्स की अदालत में पेश करने का अनुरोध कर रहे हैं।

S.Kumars FILMI MUKKADAMA

n 19th October, 1975,
umars introduced this
ramme over Radio Sri Lanka
dio Ceylon) to promote
rts. It is broadcast every
day at 10.30 a.m.

dio Sri Lanka programmes
eamed to many countries of
world: Malaysia, Singapore,
g Kong, West Asia, Egypt,
ritius, Fiji and some African
ntries. It also reaches
al and Bhutan.

ry soon with the help of a
erful new transmitter, listeners
ngland and Central Europe
be able to tune in as well.
programme is export
ted and is gaining popularity
since it started.

the past, famous film
onalities have often been
viewed over the air. But for
irst time, S. Kumars have
he stars in the witness box
hear them personally answer
charges. In this unique court
an added attraction is the
esting cross-examination by
well known and inimitable,
ic prosecutor, Ameen Sayani.

addition we have introduced
iz programme on the Filmi
kadama. This interesting
ramme Quiz will be
dcast every 3 months and the
er will get a bumper prize.
first quiz programme is
duled for February 22, 1976.

day, we are receiving letters
listeners overseas as well as
dia expressing their pleasure
is programme.

Kishore Kumar: Memories of S.D. Burman
किशोर कुमार : बर्मन दा की स्मृति की चंद दुर्लभ तस्वीरें

Shabana Azmi: Film making through her eyes
शबाना आज़मी : अभिनय का नया अंकुर

Randhir Kapoor: Is film making a game?
रणधीर कपूर : फुटबाल का खेल फिल्में बनाना या पिता के
बलबूते फिल्मों में आना ?

I.S. Johar: He answered faster than he
could be questioned
आइ. एस. जौहर : हाज़िर जवाबी के दिलचस्प गौहर

Letters From Listeners

Here are translations of what some of them say:

'Your programme is good beyond words. I just can't express my appreciation, so I keep silent'...Taral Kumar, Dhanbad.

'Thank you very much for your programme, S. Kumars Filmi Mukkadama. We sincerely feel that one day it will be the best programme on the air'...Abani Kanta, Orissa.

'Every week about 25 to 30 people meet in my house to listen to your programme. I have to serve them tea. I think I should bill you for increasing my expenses by presenting such a good programme!'...Virendra Kalsi, Bhatinda.

We are receiving numerous requests from the listeners to feature their favourite stars and film personalities like: Dilip Kumar, Dev Anand, Rajesh Khanna, Sanjeev Kumar, Dharmendra, Hema Malini, Rekha, Jaya, Rishi Kapoor, Sunil Dutt, Asha Parekh, Helen, and Johnny Walker.

Getting stars in and interviewing them was the done thing; putting them in the dock in an imaginary courtroom and interrogating them in a mock accusatory manner, was quite another. It was a format that could pique public curiosity and interest.

'We approached both Hamid and Ameen Sayani at Radio Ceylon,' Sista says, 'but they said they could not take on any advertising related programme not created by them.' So Sista hired a studio and set about crafting the programme on his own.

Sista remembers that Dicky Rutnagar, the cricketer, used to have a programme on the rest day of the five-day cricket Test Matches, where he would interview cricketers. The plan was to slot in the 'Mukkadama' as a mid-test special.

Once the initial episodes were ready, a slot had to be found to air it. And sponsors too.

When Sista approached Dilip Piramal of VIP, who was also his client, Piramal showed little inclination in sponsoring the radio show. Sista next thought of S.Kumars. And Abhay Kumar was interested. 'He was very enthusiastic,' Sista says, 'and the programme went on air.' Rutnagar, a very popular and adroit commentator on cricket, who would have 300 matches to his credit by his retirement, would conduct the interrogation. The programme featured star cricketers. 'I invited Ameen Sayani to create radio spots for S.Kumars,' he says, adding that he still has memories of trudging up the narrow steps to Sayani's office in Cecil Court in South Bombay's Colaba Causeway.

When Rutnagar migrated to England, the 'Mukkadama' show took on a new avatar. In 1975, on October 19, the 'S.Kumars Filmi Mukkadama' would be aired for the first time over Radio Ceylon. The voice of the interrogator was a familiar one to listeners who loved his easy, friendly manner and his facility with words ... Ameen Sayani.

Ramesh Laddha, an integral part of the S.Kumars marketing team, who worked closely with Ameen Sayani on the programme, says it was very easy for him to get the singers and stars on board. 'Ameen Bhai was well known to most of them, and we were giving

AMEEN SAYANI

WITH HIRALAL DUSSANE

WITH AMITABH BACHCHAN

WITH VINOD SHARMA

WITH S.S. VASAN

BRANDS DO NOT MATTER, THE PEOPLE WORKING BEHIND THE BRAND DO. A PERSONAL TOUCH IS MOST IMPORTANT IN BUSINESS.

– SHAMBHU KUMAR

them a wider audience,' he says, adding that Radio Ceylon was the obvious choice those days as film music had been banned on All India Radio by a government directive from B.V. Keskar, the then Minister for Information and Broadcasting, under whose charge AIR fell. Keskar had decreed that the ban would 'save' listeners from film songs which, he said, had become 'loud, erotic and westernised.'

When, a few years later the ban was lifted, Indians turned to their homegrown radio network, and Radio Ceylon lost its hold over the neighbouring country's listeners. Very naturally, S.Kumars moved the show to AIR. Ameen Sayani's voice was by now recognised by an entire nation of listeners who had been tuning in to Radio Ceylon. They moved with him to AIR. Which in turn took the S.Kumars programme, broadcast on Sundays, to every small town and village. Statistics show that the popularity of the programme, which included episodes where even the reticent Mohammad Rafi agreed to allow himself to be grilled by the compère, was matched only by Ramanand Sagar's television serial, 'Ramayan,' when it was aired years later.

With 'Filmi Mukkadama,' which went on for almost a decade, S.Kumars struck gold! The tens of thousands of postcards they received every week filled with appreciative messages, was evidence of the show's success. The show paled a bit, when some stars objected to featuring in a 'Filmi Mukkadama,' and Sayani changed it to 'Filmi Mulakaat.'

'Both Bhaiya Saheb and Dada Saheb knew the power of the radio,' Laddha

says. 'But when television came in, radio suffered a terrible drop in the number of listeners.'

It was a very confusing time. Television was obviously the medium of the future. But it was fiercely expensive, with producers and the government wanting to make the most of its potential. S.Kumars continued with radio, promoting their new products, but kept their antennae up for possibilities to bend the new medium to their needs.

The idea of sponsoring 'Chitrahaar' was a daring one. Laddha says, 'it was a pioneering thought spearheaded by Shobha Doctor. She had won her laurels as the producer of India's first popular soap … "Humlog," which had entranced Indian watchers.' Doctor now pushed the idea of a sponsored programme on television.

Laddha remembers that he made 'countless trips back and forth between Bombay and Delhi, to meet a Mr. Gill at Doordarshan.' Both Abhay Kumar and Shambhu Kumar would keep abreast of every change in mood, and development in the route to getting the permissions required to add their name as the first ever sponsors to a television show. Finally, the due nods were given, and the programme, sponsored by S.Kumars went on air. It would be beamed every Wednesday.

Ameen Sayani would introduce the programme. To him was given too, the task of selecting the songs to be shown. 'Chitrahaar,' that started as a programme for housewives to view at three pm, soon moved to the prime time slot of seven pm.

ABHAY KUMAR WITH SHAMBHU KUMAR

AMEEN SAYANI

WITH RAMESH LADDHA & TEAM | NEERJA VILLA | INDORE

AMEEN SAYANI WITH NANDA | STUDIO A | BOMBAY

MEHDI HASSAN | AMEEN SAYANI'S DESK | BOMBAY

MEHDI HASAN | TALKING TO A LISTENER

The S.Kumars logo and jingle would play at the start and end of the episode. Doordarshan, as against the 2200 rupees for the half hour 'Filmi Mukkadama' slot, charged an amount that started at one lakh rupees per episode. And grew three-fold.

Once again, a nation of listeners and watchers was held in thrall. The publicity the brand wrested from this was huge. S.Kumars had struck gold yet again! By the second week the S.Kumars jingle was recognised by the entire nation. The programme brought in viewers who had not tuned in to the radio show.

S.Kumars sponsored 'Chitrahaar' for three-and-a-half years. Till Doordarshan realised that the programme was a golden egg that they should use for themselves. When the rates were pushed up, the Group bowed out. Despite a 15-week slot opened for new bidders, no takers showed up to make their offer. The golden egg proved to be just gilt for DD. And the show went down in memory as an S.Kumars show.

Even as they mined the air waves to persuade the country to change to synthetic fabrics, Shambhu Kumar continued his on-ground wooing of his dealers. Sangle remembers that posters and calendars would go out to dealers, accompanied by personally addressed letters. The calendars were attractive and in a size that made them easy to hang in the shops so the brand recognition was subtle but constant through the year.

No corner was missed in the attempt to be known and recognised. Shambhu Kumar, with his brother, Abhay Kumar, had taken the idea that he had launched tremulously just over three decades ago, and built it into a powerhouse of a brand that had touched a new horizon in textiles.

The time was ripe for newer conquests. ⊛

TURNING INDUSTRIALIST IN THE '70s

S hambhu Kumar bought Dilkhush Dyeing in Andheri, in North Bombay, in 1976, and turned it into SKM Fabrics. There is an eloquent story connected with the purchase of his first commercial property that lends an insight into Shambhu Kumar's thinking and philosophy.

He remembers the scene vividly. 'We were two brothers, facing four or five *seths* who were the owners. There were some middlemen, too. I watched the middlemen huddled in whispered conversation with the *seths*. I stood before them with folded hands and said, "How much do you expect, how much do you want to sell at?" They replied, 25 lakhs. I gave them 2525000, and said, "Give me your blessing that this must go on growing."' Everyone left happy. Obviously, the blessings had the desired effect.

Starting with no formal education worth its name and with no technical knowledge,

Shambhu Kumar was fortunate to have come across accomplished individuals in his sojourn through the various companies and manufacturing units … individuals who would provide him the technical acumen to catapult his S.Kumars into a full-fledged diversified textile manufacturing powerhouse. With this expansion trail, he was well on his way to becoming an industrialist.

As Chairman, Shambhu Kumar quickly moved to convert the processing unit to work on suitings, emboldened by M.S. Hardikar, a well-entrenched administrator-cum-technician at Kamal Dyeing. Hardikar put together the entire team for Shambhu Kumar to get this activity going, and also provided the much needed start-up management. They added two new German machines to the existing one and launched processing. Running 24 hours into three shifts they increased the production from one batch a shift to

10 a day. 'The total overhead cost was divided over 10 batches from three,' as Om Prakash Pacheria, who was then hands-on in production, pointed out.

Shambhu Kumar would oversee every process at every stage. 'We worked to produce more, improve the dyeing techniques and results, and our own work style,' he adds.

'A lot of trial and error went into our processes, but we sorted it out, ensuring no fabric was wasted or spoilt.'

Shambhu Kumar motivated his team by offering a profit sharing model of payment. 'My Assistant Dyeing Master, Engineer, the Accountant and myself would get around 1-2 per cent of the profit the company made. When Kaka's son, Vikas, took over, he increased the profit participation to 10 per cent,' he adds. 'I was granted 60 per cent of the 10 per cent, and the remaining was shared proportionately among the rest of my team.' It was a great incentive indeed, and the output rose phenomenally, to the ultimate capacity of both man and machine. 'In one year, I earned 4-5 lakhs over and above my salary,' Pacheria remembers.

The next year, in 1977, 'when Kaka felt we must have a factory near Indore, construction from the ground up of the Dewas processing house would swing into action,' Pacheria says. He was commissioned to put up the plant. 'It was a big project, I started spending 15 days every month at Dewas and the rest in running SKM Fabrics.'

He explains that the mercerising process was undertaken to give cotton cloth a sheen. 'We set up a mercerising machine. The wet fabric would be brought here, washed in the jigger, dyed, finished and sent to market. Everything was done with clockwork precision. Profitability rose markedly.'

Other decisions would make a considerable difference to profits too. When Dewas started production, the suiting material was moved there, so we took up job work, which was hugely profitable. We dyed double the metres per shade per batch instead of the 1000 metres most others did in a batch. We had a shade chart, clients would choose from it, and we would entertain orders even for small quantities. I would take orders from three parties if need be, to attain the batch size for that particular shade. We would run 2000 metres in one shift. And I would charge a small premium of between 25 to 50 paise per metre.

This timely decision of doing job work added to the productivity and optimum use of the machines. 'We built up a name for dependability,' Pacheria remembers, 'and the orders grew. The greige cloth we got was in huge quantities, which we would store in the neighbouring Modak Rubber Products Factory.'

Small incidents show how problems could affect even the best run companies, and how solving them showed the true mettle of the people at the helm.

Pacheria tells the story. 'We were dyeing olive green cloth for the Army at Dewas. The packing was being done at the Kamal Enterprises premises in the Marol, MIDC area. The MIDC staff believed in work to rule, and would leave at 5 pm. When the

Defence people came to take their goods, there was no one, as all the workmen had left.

'This was not good. I decided to give the contract of packing of the material to Modak Rubber agency instead. I consulted Vikas Babu, who gave his approval, and the material was shifted.

'Every evening I would go from the factory in Andheri to the office at Niranjan Building to discuss the day with Vikas Babu. Kaka happened to be passing by when he heard the word *union* being discussed by us. "What about union?" he asked, and I explained about the Defence order packing. Somehow, Kaka flew into a rage and shouted at Vikas Babu, saying he had taken a wrong decision. Though the decision had been mine, and he had only okayed it, Vikas Babu kept quiet, taking the flak. But I could not keep quiet. I turned to Kaka. "Is it that only what you say is right?" I asked. "What do you mean," asked Kaka, surprised. "Listen to me," I responded, "Do I not have the right to speak? I cannot let my Defence commitments suffer, even if I have to work through the entire night to keep to it," I explained, "so I sought and found a solution."

'Kaka was quiet for a few long seconds, and I held my breath. Then he

'HAVAN' DEWAS

MY FAVOURITE HOBBY IS BUSINESS, BUSINESS AND GOOD BUSINESS. WHEN BUSINESS IS SUCCESSFUL YOU ENJOY IT TOO.

– SHAMBHU KUMAR

looked at me and said quietly, "You are right. I accept I was wrong." That was that.

'The next day, I went to him and apologised, but he said, "You are right." I said, "But I spoke in a very undisciplined way, I am sorry." He replied, "I have only yes men around me, I do not always see mistakes when they happen. This message that you gave had to be given in the language and manner you used, to have effect." Anyway, I apologised once again and left. I worried if the incident would have repercussions.

It did. His confidence in me grew and boosted me.

'I learned everything an IIM could have taught me, here,' he adds, 'I don't think even at a Management School, I would have picked up some of the things I learned here.'

By 1978, Shambhu Kumar had acquired one of the largest composite textile mills on the Indian firmament. The Shree Ram Mills was an ailing mill with 6000 staff. It

was a huge liability, but it was a prestigious mill as it specialised in superfine cotton fabrics like rubia, voiles, and was known for its dhotis. It also produced tracing fabric, an industrial fabric used for engineering procedures.

No one knows where the rumour began, 'but it was floated that S.Kumars was going bankrupt,' says Shambhu Kumar's son, Vikas. 'Fortunately, my father and uncle handled it all diplomatically and deftly and no damage was done.'

TEAM S.KUMARS | INDUSTRIAL COMPLEX | PITHAMPUR

SHAMBHU KUMAR & PROCESSING TEAM WITH WARIJ & NITIN

'LAXMI POOJAN' BY AMBUJ | VITHALWADI OFFICE

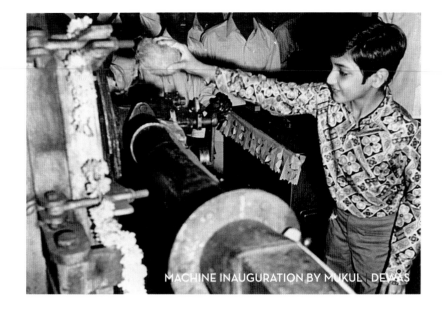

MACHINE INAUGURATION BY MUKUL, DEWAS

PRODUCTION LAUNCH | SHAMBHU KUMAR, VIKAS, RAJKUMARI & WORKERS

The company also found that dealers stood solidly by its side. Though the rumour was untrue, dealers sent in money, 'and our bank balance tripled, thanks to the inflow,' Vikas says. 'Luckily, they also had the trust of the seller, and CAFI too stood solidly behind them and the deal went through.'

It was later learnt that the rumour had been started by someone who was keen on buying the mill, and wanted to break the deal that was being made between the mill owners and S.Kumars.

'My father was extremely courteous to the owners of the mill he had acquired. He insisted that Bhogilal Leherchand, who had been the owner, should continue as the Chairman, and his son, Pratap Bhogilal, who had been the MD, should have some role to play in the company for some time,' Vikas adds.

Though they eventually closed the tracing fabric section, the mill continued to produce superfine cotton varieties, adding high value cottons to the S.Kumars arsenal. The mill would handle every operation from spinning to processing under its spreading roofs.

Within a short time, through the fine marketing practices and the dealer network they had set up, S.Kumars managed to turn around the sick mill and profits started rolling in.

The credit for this also goes to R.N. Joshi, an experienced and well qualified textile technician from the Killick Nixon-Kohinoor Mills foray, who took over the reins of Shree Ram Mills on behalf of Shambhu Kumar and steered it out of the woods. RNJ, as he was fondly known to all, was ably assisted by Shambhu Kumar's older brother, Abhay Kumar. RNJ would go on to become one of the most trusted people in Shambhu Kumar's coterie, more than a family member and one who would help and guide Shambhu Kumar through various challenges, whether business or personal.

Shubh Karan Luharuka remembers the high point in his career with the S.Kumars Group. 'I started in 1987 with Shree Ram Mills and S.Kumars as a Marketing Manager. In one year, I was promoted to GM and two years later, as President of the company.' Such was the prestige and exposure of holding a high position with the Group that 'I was appointed a Director of Indian Bank by the Government of India. I learnt a lot while looking after Shree Ram Mills and all the S.Kumars companies,' he adds.

Shree Ram Mills was proving to be a sound investment for S.Kumars. But when

Datta Samant started his strike, Shree Ram Mills reeled under the attack, like every other mill in Bombay. The strike hit the textile industry hard; and though the mill went back into production sporadically, it never really recovered.

Shree Ram Mills shut down finally in 1994. 'In 1996, after the 6000 employees were sent off through VRS, I was shifted to S.Kumars Nationwide Ltd. (SKNL), to look after the Dewas plant. Nitin Babu was the MD and Kaka was the Chairman. Through the end of the millennium, till 2006, I was given charge as Executive Director to look after all the new plants that were coming up,' he says. Luharuka adds that through the many positions he served the company in, a constant was the fact that everyone was appreciative of his work and did not hold back on letting good performance go unnoticed. Promotions and increments came unreservedly. 'Anyone who has served with the Group can vouch for this,' he says. Luharuka also appreciated the fact that unlike in most other mills, Shambhu Kumar's granddaughter, Dhvani was appointed a director in Shree Ram Mills. 'I don't know many other companies who would appoint a young woman on the board; it shows the forward-thinking nature of the Group,' he says. ◉

THE ROTARY SPIRIT

When Shambhu Kumar founded the Rotary Club of Bombay South in 1971, as one of its Charter Members, he became a Rotarian in the true sense of the word. In the service organisation, he found an echo of his own principles and values.

The four main tenets of the Rotary organisation are to provide service to others, promote integrity, and advance world understanding, goodwill, and peace through its fellowship of business, professional, and community leaders. Truth, integrity and concern for lesser privileged human beings is high on the Club's list of values.

'It was a perfect environment for someone like him,' says Shyam Sundar Kejriwal, a fellow businessman and Rotarian. Both were part of the same Chapter. Kejriwal found Shambhu Kumar 'very understanding and cooperative. A good friend and a good human being.' Kejriwal would meet him once or twice a month 'and we became friends beyond Rotary too; our friendship spans 15 years.'

As President of the Rotary Club in 1977-78, Shambhu Kumar initiated many projects that would be carried on long after he handed over the post to his successor. They were sound projects, successfully implemented. 'He showed the way forward, so others followed,' Kejriwal says.

In his acceptance speech as President, Shambhu Kumar highlighted the fact that Rotarians needed to be present, and involved in the projects of the Chapter. Emphasising

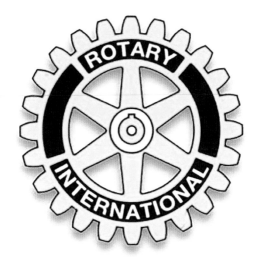

the importance and indispensability of 'participation' as an integral part of Rotary, he said, 'I do believe in this very seriously and sincerely. In fact, if I were asked to sum up all my expectations from fellow-members during my tenure as President into just one word, what I would readily say is: Participation. Because that is the cornerstone of Rotary. Without participation by its members, Rotary becomes just like any other charitable institution. And Rotary is *not* like any other charitable institution. It has a distinct and distinguishing concept of service of its own which is manifest in the requirement that every service that Rotary renders should spring from the active and personal involvement in it of its members. The most important person in any Rotary Club is the individual Rotarian, i.e. You.' His speech had the necessary effect. Attendance at the Club spiked to 90 per cent!

Expanding on the theme of participation and involvement, he would add in a later speech, 'Rotary invests an added dimension to service by insisting that the Rotarians should be directly and personally involved in and associated with all their service activities; thus establishing a meaningful contact between the contributor and the recipient. This way a Rotarian learns to uphold the dignity and value inherent in every human being, and in the process, himself becomes a better person: enlightened, aware, concerned and in touch with the realities of life and existence around him.'

Some of the key projects that were initiated by Shambhu Kumar during his tenure are remembered to this present day. They included providing entertainment and good company for the aged, installing a library of old magazines at hospitals, remand houses and the Arthur Road Jail; free ENT and medical check-up at Our Lady of Dolours Church. He was especially happy when Interactors of St. Xavier's Boys' Academy collected more than 2000 rupees within a week and donated articles like bed sheets, pillow cases, trolleys and some eatables to the institute run by the Sisters of Mother Teresa.

And it was during Shambhu Kumar's presidency that Justice M.C. Chagla became the first ever Honorary Rotarian. His Royal Highness Prince Karim Aga Khan, the Imam of the Islamic community, attended the joint meeting of the Rotary Clubs of Bombay as the chief guest.

Shambhu Kumar was particularly happy when he got the cloth dealers involved in the Rotary movement by convincing them to donate blood. On 13th December 1977, over 45 bottles of blood were collected from people in the *kapda* market as donation!

SHAMBHU KUMAR WITH OUTGOING PRESIDENT RATU BHAI MASRANI

JUSTICE M.C. CHAGLA MADE HONORARY MEMBER

WITH SURENDRA MEHTA & BAPU SAHEB
BHORGAY | DISTRICT ASSEMBLY

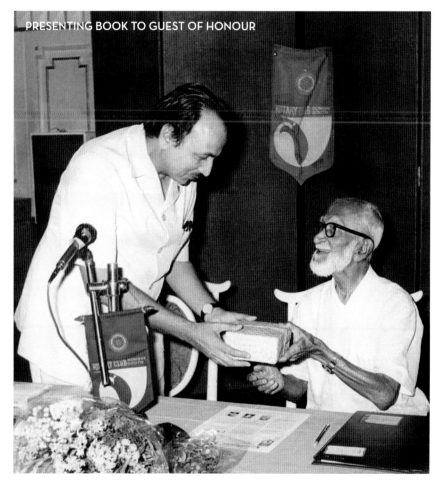

PRESENTING BOOK TO GUEST OF HONOUR

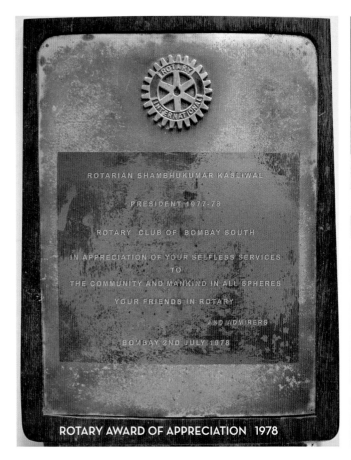

ROTARY AWARD OF APPRECIATION 1978

SHAMBHU KUMAR ATTENDING ROTARY MEETING WITH OTHER MEMBERS

WHEN IGNORANCE IS BLISS, IT IS FOOLISH TO BE WISE.

– SHAMBHU KUMAR

AT ROTARY CLUB PICNIC | 1975

Kejriwal was struck by the philanthropic streak in Shambhu Kumar. He mentions the fact that his friend donates generously every year to the Club's causes, as well as to the Rotary International, to use for their projects in other countries. 'He won't talk about it, but he makes a hefty donation to the Rotary Foundation every year, at least for the years I have known him as a fellow Rotarian,' he adds.

The two men with their better halves have travelled together, on many of Shambhu Kumar's much-loved road trips. Kejriwal remembers that Shambhu Kumar extended an invitation to the members of Rotary Club to visit Indore and hosted 25 to 30 Rotarians and their families for three days, sparing no effort to give them hospitality fit for princes.

Perhaps his experience and his innate understanding of men and matters helped. Kejriwal says, 'He would often be the one everyone turned to for solving a knotty situation.'

There were many instances where, 'Shambhu Kumar ji spoke up with the wisdom of a Solomon.' Little wonder that the Club graced him with the title of 'Bhishma Pitamah,' he says, adding, 'he is the only member to be thus honoured.' As Rajkumari pointed out, 'He always had 100 per cent attendance, year after year. When he had his bypass, he had the meeting venue shifted to our house! He did not want to lose his record.

'It took a kidney transplant to break his all-time attendance record of 100 per cent, otherwise he has been attending meetings week after week, all over the world, whether he was in a remote town in South India or in a city in Southern California, for the last 50 years!' she adds. Believe it or not, he attended meetings on Zoom during the Covid-19 period.

'Everyone only has respect for him,' Kejriwal says, 'and he knows each member well, and remains in close contact with all. Despite his professional preoccupations and family commitments, he remains a true Rotarian, and is one in spirit as well as in deeds. I doubt any of the Rotary Clubs have many others with the same level of commitment to the Club.'

It's common for newly inducted Presidents and Governors of various Rotary Clubs to meet Shambhu Kumar to seek his blessings for a good term in office. ⑤

ENJOYING THE NEWSPAPER PAPER FOLD | ROTARY GAME NIGHT

THE NATURE OF NURTURE

SHAMBHU KUMAR WITH GRANDCHILDREN

Through the 1980s, the Kasliwal household would resound with the patter of tiny feet and the prattle of childish voices. 1981 saw the birth of Shambhu Kumar's first grandchild, Vikas' daughter, Vidhi. A second daughter, Dhvani, would follow two years later, in 1983. The family kept growing steadily, with Anjani, Nitin's daughter, born in 1986 and the first grandson, Kartikeya in 1988.

Bent now on strengthening what would soon be known as the S.Kumars Group, Shambhu Kumar built a warp knitting unit in 1984, and named it after his granddaughter: Dhvani Terefabs Exports Pvt. Ltd. It was an idea mooted by N.L. Longani who was keen to work on warp knitting. Lalit Bhatt, currently Director, Manufacturing, at the Dhvani Terefabs weaving factory traces the process of setting up the unit. He was already a casual employee of the Group since 1982, and when work in the new factory started, he was transferred to it as factory manager. 'When I joined, I said in response to Kaka's question, "I can do anything," and I think he realised I meant it. Kaka has the knack of looking at a person's face and understanding his potential,' Bhatt says.

And sure enough, he was soon 'doing everything.' 'I obtained the machines, looked after production, sales, export, overseeing it all,' he says. 'At that time no one understood knitted towels; we introduced it in Madhya Pradesh, and with Lalaram as a co-agent, toured the State to sell. It was an uphill task; we needed to push hard,' he recollects.

'We got our machines from Germany; in 1984 the first one was erected. Three years later, a second machine followed, and yet another was installed in 1996.' By this time, after his stint as a student in Rochester, the youngest son, Mukul joined. 'Both Kaka and Kaki would come every time the machines were being erected.'

The machines were piquantly named, Ganga, Jamuna and Kaveri. 'We have the only machines for warp knitted towels in India,' he avers. The advantage of warp knitted towels, vis a vis the regular woven ones, is that the former dries easily, and are light to carry on travels. The concept was new in India. Warp knitted towels are different from woven ones in that there is no weft, and they have a small polyester component. Not surprisingly, the towels found a huge market in Calcutta; perhaps due to its humid climate and long rainy seasons.

Bhatt shares the modus operandi of running the factories in Dewas. 'We had a zero hour, during which anyone could ask any question,' he says. 'It made a huge impact on creating a family feeling, of ensuring the inclusion of the workers into the Kasliwal fold. During zero hour, discussions would be plenty, but always without prejudice or rancour.' The rules also included the fact that everyone ate together in the canteen.

Bhatt still ensures that there are combs and mirrors kept for the workers to use before they go home, 'mainly as we have a lot of women in the weaving unit,' he says. 'We also choose four Star Workers every month and put up their photos. It's a great feel-good factor for all.' Bhatt got the idea from the 'page in Kaka's book that one must let workers get ahead and help them. And know their stories personally.'

Bhatt, who says Shambhu Kumar has always addressed him as Bhatt ji, adds that the senior would let him take the lead and guide him in the buying of both, the spinning and the weaving machines. 'I was a non-technical man, but he made a tech-man out of me,' he says with a smile. 'He would explain in detail how to manufacture, how to sell. He would guide me through the P&L meetings held every month. He did have a fiery temper and could flare up if he found errors, or if I made a mistake which happened in the early years; but he would cool down instantly too. I made sure soon enough there would be no occasion for him to lose his temper. We would spend time discussing all social, political issues that went beyond the work I did. Now, as my office is upstairs, he is planning for a lift to be put in, so he can come and sit with me and resume our chats over tea.'

Through the decades, the S.Kumars Group would establish several weaving units in Bombay and Dewas ranging from the conventional shuttle looms to the latest air jet machines, including the automatic CIMMCO looms, that would be imported and installed.

Talking about Shambhu Kumar's initiatives in setting up units, Kamal Kishore Maini has vivid memories of his role in the process.

IT'S THE ESSENCE OF LIFE; DO GOOD BUT DON'T EXPECT ANYTHING IN RETURN. EXPECTATIONS WILL CAUSE NOTHING BUT SADNESS. TODAY WHAT SEEMS AS SACRIFICE, TOMORROW CHANGES INTO INVESTMENT.

– SHAMBHU KUMAR

THE KASLIWAL FAMILY | NEERJA VILLA | INDORE

Maini has seen its growth first-hand from a simple weaving unit to a complex of mills that produce diverse textile ranges.

Moving to Dewas from Faridabad in the early 1970s, he first joined Dewas Textiles Pvt. Ltd. as General Manager under Jawaharlal Daga, who was the Managing Director. 'We were producing greige fabric and supplying it for processing and dyeing.' His job included carrying the material to Bombay, getting it processed, and bringing it back to pack and sell. When Shambhu Kumar decided to set up a processing unit and do the dyeing themselves, Maini was the man he chose to handle the project.

Maini spent two years waiting for the new factory to start coming up, overseeing everything from the Kasliwal residence in Indore in the meantime. Shifting to the factory site, then, he set about getting things moving. 'There was no roof over our head,' he remembers, 'I had a chair, a Godrej table and an almirah; but work started.' He recruited non-textile labour and trained them, 'all construction workers

were soon running the show,' he says. 'A foreman was picked, and every recruit was placed under him for training. If someone fell short or showed no interest or potential, he could choose another. The process was continuous. In the beginning, there was a lot of turnover of trained men. People from Bhilwara, presently the country's biggest textile hub for suitings, would drive up in a Matador and poach our men, fit 25 of them into the van and drive off. We would have to pick replacements for them and start training all over again. In due course, our workers learned the benefit of staying on.

'Today,' he adds, 'none of our semi-skilled workers are lesser than their counterparts in other companies. Many of the current employees are second generation employees who have joined the factory their fathers started in.'

Maini says that though Shambhu Kumar's sons, especially Vikas, were also involved, 'whenever Kaka Saheb would come, I would do the rounds with him. He never missed a visit.'

'Such was his nature that if I was not at work because of some ill health, he would not go to the factory in my absence. He would wait for me to resume and go with me. Which owner gives an employee so much respect?'

As with most of his team members, Shambhu Kumar developed a culture of mutual trust. 'He would give me a cheque book with signed leaves, and leave the last leaf unsigned. I was the counter signatory. When I needed a fresh one, I would send the booklet back with the last leaf intact, and the stubs would tell him how the monies had been disbursed. It was pure diplomacy at work, so we did not have to discuss money or my decisions about it. He never asked me, or worried over the unsigned leaf in my custody.'

Currently CEO of the Group, Subhash Kataria has been with the company since August 25, 1985, when he had joined as Sales Officer in Dewas, handling marketing and production on behalf of the Head Office in Bombay. 'Kaka Saheb interviewed me. I had an MBA in Marketing from Indore so I was told to base myself in Dewas,' he remembers. The modus operandi followed would be that Nitin would pass on the dealer information that came to Bombay Head Office to Kataria, with details of quality of fabric, colour, finish and shade required. 'My job was to plan the production for the month, and distribute the jobs to weaving, processing and other units. All of it with constant approvals from Nitin Babu.'

Kataria says that he learnt more from his mentor, 'Kaka Saheb,' than his MBA Degree had taught him. 'Kaka is the master of marketing, he takes pains and time to guide,' Kataria says. And lists some of the tenets shared by his mentor that he himself follows:

1. Our word has to be followed through 100 per cent. If Subhash Kataria has said it in the market, and we find it is a mistake that will cost us, it still must be followed. We never go back on a given word.

2. Think first. Before speaking, acting.

3. No one has the authority to compromise on quality whatever be the situation. Quality has to be strictly maintained.

   'This is how we have maintained the same quality for the past 75 years,' Kataria says, 'even if the competition copies they cannot compete, as the count of yarn we use is different from what is in the market. Our margins remain better too, as we have three ranges: Economy, mid-range and high-end.'

4. The price remains constant across all of the country, in all situations; though an order of a huge quantity may be open to a token discount.

5. Do not by-pass the dealer. He is important and we must keep faith in our dealers. They are our customers, and they need to trust us. When, and if, direct contact with the end user is required, then take the dealer along.

   Kataria gives an example of this: 'We received a large order from the Hero Motor Corporation. We told them, we have a dealer in Delhi, please come through him. When the dealer said he was unable to handle the load due to some personal problem, we appointed another dealer. But still gave the previous one a percentage.'

6. Whichever wholesalers we fix, are only appointed with the consent of the agent. So, he knows the cycle of activities regarding supply and payments.

7. Keep the scheme going. For dealers paying on Day 10, three per cent discount; Day 20, two per cent, Day 30, one per cent. From bill to bill, he allowed 45 days. After that he would levy interest at seven paise per 100 rupees per day. As Kataria puts it, 'The scheme worked wonders.'

   The full season for sales is from October to May. Three months, between July and September, would be off-season, and 'Kaka found a way to keep the sales going through the lag. He would offer a dealer incentive of one per cent if a dealer in the smaller regions took 21 cases of material. It would be a special allowance included in the bill. In the bigger South Indian markets, the one per cent would be offered for 101 cases, going up to four per cent for larger orders.'

8. Finish every job immediately. Nothing is ever pending on his table. He deals with everything, then and there.

9. Time is money. If I was late by five minutes, he would point to the clock and say, "Understand the value of time." He himself would always be five minutes early.

10. Treat dealers and agents as family. Book a room in a hotel for him, send a car to receive him. You would do it for your family and he is family.

    Kataria adds that in spite of being the ultimate authority at the All India Dealer Meets, Shambhu Kumar would have a steering council of 10-12 main agents and plan the agenda with them. He would take their advice on schemes, on how to implement them, how to increase sales.

11. Never take loans. *Jitni razai, utne pair phailao,* he always said. Borrowings lose you respect in the market.

CELEBRATION LUNCH

STAFF CRICKET MATCH

GOLDEN ANNIVERSARY OF S.KUMARS

persuaded his elder brother to be the face of the Group. Abhay Kumar would embark on a long and prestigious journey through business politics, holding numerous offices of distinction, including Chairman of the Maharashtra Chamber of Commerce and Chairman of The Synthetic and Rayon Textiles Export Promotion Council (SRTEPC). Abhay Kumar came in close contact with O.P. Dhawan in SRTEPC. Dhawan proved to be a big anchor for both the brothers. Being well-versed in the management of business associations, Dhawan was also instrumental in Abhay Kumar becoming President of FICCI.

And realising that his wife was lonely once his daughter Neerja married and moved into her new family's home, Shambhu Kumar persuaded Rajkumari to take on an enterprise of her own, and run it with complete authority and confidence. By early 1990, Rajkumari, till then wife, mother, grandmother and home manager and her husband's soulmate, would add one more descriptor to her name: that of turning around the towel factory, managing it all on her own, from start to finish. ⊚

Kataria credits Shambhu Kumar with a special ability to teach by example. 'No one can teach like him. If you go to his cabin with a problem and say, "we are stuck," within five minutes, he will come up with a suggestion that would be so simple that we would wonder why we did not think of it.'

According to Kataria, he has never seen 'an industrialist like Kaka Saheb. He is an organisation unto himself.' He

avers, 'An expert in finance, marketing, manufacturing. And it is all self-taught.' Shambhu Kumar is also known to make copious notes on all the meetings and happenings. He has countless diaries filled with his thoughts and feelings to refer to whenever needed.

A reticent man more interested in the nitty gritty of all aspects of his business, Shambhu Kumar

ABHAY KUMAR WITH DIGNITARIES & BUSINESS LEADERS

ABHAY KUMAR, BY SHEER DINT OF HIS INTELLIGENCE AND COMMUNICATION SKILLS, WENT FROM STRENGTH TO STRENGTH IN THE WORLD OF BUSINESS AND SOCIAL ASSOCIATIONS.

A TOUCH OF LOVE

Like every mother, who feels the emptiness of the nest when a daughter marries and leaves the home she has been cocooned in through her growing years, Rajkumari felt herself somewhat adrift. The boys were men now, with lives and interests and families of their own. Her husband, whom she looked after, watching over his health with an eagle's eye, remained her priority, but she was used to doing so much more. Neerja had been a sunny presence in her life, a girl to share womanly talk with, to shape and tend so she would blossom into a graceful, lovely woman capable of holding her own and steering her own way in life. 'Now, with her marriage, it was as if a vacuum had taken over the space my daughter had occupied' Rajkumari says.

When her husband suggested she take on the running of the towelling factory, Rajkumari accepted the idea without a moment's hesitation. It was decided that she would be the sole decision maker in all matters concerning the operations of the unit in Dewas. And it would be an autonomous unit and have its own P&L. To her credit, she came up with the 'Dhvani Love Touch' branding.

'Kaki runs the factory like she runs her home,' says Rajendra Mehta, who also happens to be Rajkumari's sister's husband. 'There are none of the business tricks that many units practise; here in Kaki's factory, everyone is like a family member. She exercises the same prudence and economy that she exercises in running her household.

'Kaki took charge of everything from planning to production; working out the plans in Bombay and sending the details to us here to execute.' Rajendra Mehta continues, 'The entire culture was different. Though there were the machines that knitted the towels, and men operated them, Kaki drew a woman's workforce into the unit. Today 90 per cent of its employees are women.'

Lokendra Bakliwal, who joined the Group in 2000, was handed charge of purchase, sale and banking for Dhvani Love Touch. 'My dad was on good terms with Kaka and when Kaka said I could join whenever I wanted, I did so, as quickly as possible. I was told to assist Kaki. That's what I still do, besides other tasks.'

Under Rajkumari's direct supervision, Bakliwal purchases yarn and takes care of much of the rest. 'I am involved when spare parts are to be imported for the knitting machines; our three machines, Ganga, Jamuna, Kaveri, produce 30 tonnes of ready towelling material a month. In addition, we have eight looms that weave towels, and produce 8-9 tonnes a month. I have to ensure there is no hitch in their functioning.'

Bakliwal says that now the unit has broadened its scope to include making slippers for hotel rooms, bathrobes, hair bands, napkins and car seat covers, all of which have found a ready market.

'I take up whatever work Kaki assigns me,' Bakliwal says. 'We have permission to call her anytime, even at night, if there is a problem that needs her attention or advice.'

He adds that she is, 'exacting, and will demand prompt follow-ups. If she asks me something and I do not immediately respond, she will pick up the phone and call. Without fail, Kaki phones me every morning at 8.45, and keeps abreast of what is happening in her unit. Thanks to her, I have learnt a lot; my own method of working has improved,' he says. 'But make no mistake about it, she is as soft hearted as she is sharp and disciplined. I have many instances I can share about this soft side of her personality.'

Whenever she visits Dewas, which is often, Rajkumari takes stock of the unit

under her care. But it is not just the P&L and the machine maintenance or other such technical aspects, that come under her scrutiny. 'She will meet the women, sit with them, listen to their stories, and try to solve any problems they may present to her, concerning the work space, or even beyond it. She was never into the hire and fire mode, instead has an open-door policy and tries to work out an issue with a worker if it comes up. Needless to say, she looks into every aspect of the manufacturing, keeping up-to-date with production, and marketing.'

Perhaps what makes Rajkumari the perfect manager are some management practices she follows.

1. She is super-efficient because she is a quick decision maker.

2. She never mixes personal and business money. Pays for every piece of towel she may pick up for the home or as a gift.

3. She deals with her staff with compassion as human beings and not just statistics.

And indeed, a walk through the towelling factory shows up the feminine side of the S.Kumars enterprise. Women in gaily coloured handloom or more contemporary printed saris move around noiselessly, busy at cutting the towels that come off the loom. There is no chatter filling the air, but quiet concentration as the scissor blades rip through the margins to separate the *thaans* into individual towels. In the next room, women sit cross-legged or stand at tables stitching, folding and packing the towels, so they can be despatched. Everything seems to be in motion as they move about carrying small loads, placing them in stacks. These are tasks they are used to, and there is a joy evident that they are being paid for doing something that has been taken for granted as part of 'womanly duties' inside their own homes. Come lunch time, the mood changes as they discuss children, families, or the latest soap opera on TV.

Turnover of labour at the towel factory is low and attrition is an unknown word. In fact, her team considers their factory as their home. Which is probably why during the pandemic, they offered to sacrifice getting their salaries on time to keep the machines running as cash flows were limited. Knowing that their home fires had to be kept burning, Rajkumari found a way to balance pay-outs.

A woman at the helm makes a difference, and 'Kaki's' towelling factory is evidence of this. ◉

SONS AS STAKEHOLDERS:
Strengths And Skills

'**P**ublic perception of wealth is a hundred times the actual,' Shambhu Kumar wrote in his diary, looking back at his business in the 1980s. 'Business grows with volatility,' he adds.

Indeed, much has happened in the preceding decades that is worthy of note in the history of S.Kumar and Company. Shambhu Kumar's younger brother has branched out, 'for personal reasons.' Sumati Kumar, the man who could sell sand to a camel, has decided to trace his own future and moved back to Indore. Though he never joined the S.Kumars business again, having made his mark with his son, Manoj, in the real estate market, his ties with the family remained strong.

Despite Sumati Kumar's moving out, Shambhu Kumar took comfort not only in the fact that his brother was doing exceedingly well, but also that, 'the family remains united and disciplined.' Both are vital aspects at the moment, for the second generation of Kasliwals is on the verge of joining the business.

By the end of the '80s, Shambhu Kumar would be able to tell himself that it had been a 'total success and full of name, kudos and acceptance throughout.' He could sense 'glory everywhere.' SKNL had issued Capital and had been oversubscribed.

One by one, the boys had joined. Ambuj, Warij, Vikas and Nitin finding their niches, and Mukul too joining towards the last years of the 1980s.

To his delight, Shambhu Kumar found Mukul had the brain of a 'financial wizard.' There was much jubilation when he landed a significant term loan from IFCI; a forerunner of other such feats that would follow. While Nitin looked into the textile business, Vikas shared the planning and strategising with his father. Exports were handled by Ambuj, and Warij supported his brothers where and when required, using his multi-skills to advantage.

Abhay Kumar continued as the public face of the Group, handling business and social events with balanced élan. It's been more than 20 years since his brother's passing, but Shambhu Kumar still misses him

dearly and often gets misty-eyed thinking of their times together.

Realising that it was time to maximise the combined strengths of his family, Shambhu Kumar included his brother, nephews and sons to institute what was called a Central Management Committee. The CMC would meet once a week, every Saturday to discuss plans.

By the early '90s, the next lot of grandchildren were adding their laughter to the Kasliwal household. Vikas' sons, Arnav and Dhruv came first followed by Neerja's daughter Ananyashree and son Aryaman Vikram. The final additions to the brood were Mukul's son Vrishan and Neerja's youngest, Advaitesha.

Shambhu Kumar armed his sons with the strength of his philosophy and experiences as each began to find his chosen path in business.

He had a firm grip over his fast-growing textile empire throughout, but also stretched his borders to include other products and fields.

L TO R | WARIJ, NITIN, AMBUJ, MUKUL, VIKAS

L TO R | VIKAS, AMBUJ, NEERJA, MUKUL, SHRIJA, WARIJ, NITIN

For one, the brothers started Pankaj Tyres in Indore, a regional brand for cycle and moped tyres, which was managed by Abhay Kumar. They would also acquire Modak Rubber in Bombay and diversify into varied industrial rubber products. Abhay Kumar's younger son Warij, holding a diploma in rubber technology from London, was closely involved in Modak Rubber. S.Kumars Tyres, the unit they subsequently set up in Pithampur in Madhya Pradesh, entered into an agreement with Michelin Tyres of France to technically collaborate and make two and three-wheeler tyres under the brand name of Progard Tyres. The initiative was

spearheaded by Vikas, who was closely involved in the alignment.

It was in the 1990s that the father would provide strategic inputs and strongly support his sons Vikas and Mukul in the development of 'Maheshwar Hydel Project.' The dam across the Narmada river was planned to generate 400 megawatts of hydro-electric power that could have been an answer to the state's power outage issues.

Vikas and Mukul enthusiastically publicised their online venture,

SHAMBHU KUMAR WITH GRANDCHILDREN

'S.Kumars Online Ltd.' with an unprecedented number of hoardings all over India. It resulted in a thundering acceptance of the new idea. They had also managed to get a unique collaboration with IBM, thus creating an e-commerce platform that was way ahead of its time.

S.Kumars also succeeded in signing one of the most prestigious tie-ups made by any Indian textile company. Reid & Taylor, a brand of lightweight, superfine woollens manufactured by a Scottish company, would find its place among the most sought after woollen fabrics in India. The tie-up benefitted both partners: the Scottish company was keen to have a presence in India, and for Shambhu Kumar, it was a step into where no textile company had dared to go before. In due course, Reid & Taylor would be bought over by S.Kumars.

The woollen fabric which was soon being manufactured in Mysore, under Nitin's supervision with the involvement of Shambhu Kumar's old friend, Martin Henry, former Director of Madura Coats, was breathable and draped extremely well. It was perfectly suited to the Indian climate, in sharp contrast to the thick fabric being marketed by Raymond.

In the uncanny way he had of ensuring he projected his brands in a way that was most suitable for them, and most attractive to the target buyer, Shambhu Kumar and son Nitin,

THE GRANDCHILDREN ALL GROWN-UP

KEY PEOPLE OF S.KUMARS | L TO R SITTING | R.S. AHUJA, NARSINGHDAS GUPTA, OM PRAKASH PACHERIA, SHIRISH DALAL, KAMAL KISHORE MAINI, COL. S. RAJE, SHAMBHU KUMAR, AMBUJ KASLIWAL, NITIN KASLIWAL, WARIJ KASLIWAL, MUKUL KASLIWAL, VIKAS KASLIWAL
L TO R STANDING | R.P. SHAH, DILIP BAROT, VIROO RANGNEKAR, SUSHIL K. BIYANI, SUBHASH KATARIA, R.K. POOJARI

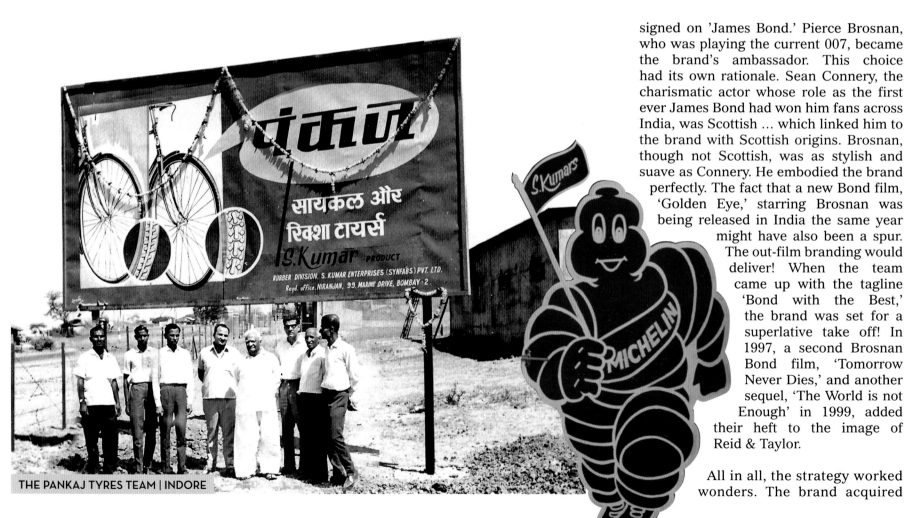

THE PANKAJ TYRES TEAM | INDORE

signed on 'James Bond.' Pierce Brosnan, who was playing the current 007, became the brand's ambassador. This choice had its own rationale. Sean Connery, the charismatic actor whose role as the first ever James Bond had won him fans across India, was Scottish ... which linked him to the brand with Scottish origins. Brosnan, though not Scottish, was as stylish and suave as Connery. He embodied the brand perfectly. The fact that a new Bond film, 'Golden Eye,' starring Brosnan was being released in India the same year might have also been a spur. The out-film branding would deliver! When the team came up with the tagline 'Bond with the Best,' the brand was set for a superlative take off! In 1997, a second Brosnan Bond film, 'Tomorrow Never Dies,' and another sequel, 'The World is not Enough' in 1999, added their heft to the image of Reid & Taylor.

All in all, the strategy worked wonders. The brand acquired

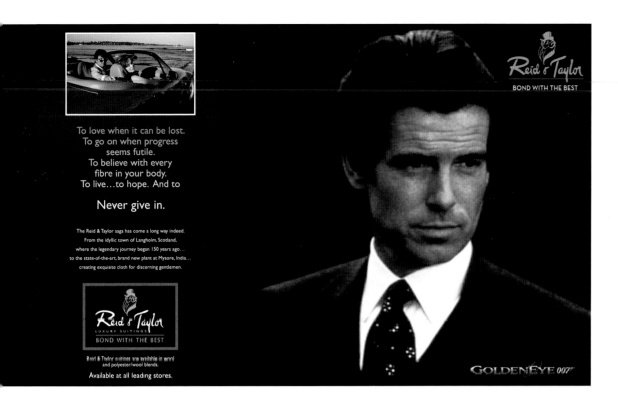

To love when it can be lost.
To go on when progress
seems futile.
To believe with every
fibre in your body.
To live…to hope. And to

Never give in.

The Reid & Taylor saga has come a long way indeed.
From the idyllic town of Langholm, Scotland,
where the legendary journey began 150 years ago…
to the state-of-the-art, brand new plant at Mysore, India…
creating exquisite cloth for discerning gentlemen.

Reid & Taylor
LUXURY SUITINGS
BOND WITH THE BEST

Reid & Taylor suitings are available in wool
and polyester/wool blends.
Available at all leading stores.

GOLDENEYE 007

AMITABH BACHCHAN WITH JYOTI KASLIWAL

THE COMPANY GREW BRANCHES IN DIFFERENT DIRECTIONS BUT I NEVER DIVERTED. THOUGH I ACCEPTED CHANGE QUICKLY, I KEPT THE FOCUS. I ONLY DID WHAT I DID BEST. AND NOTHING ELSE.

– SHAMBHU KUMAR

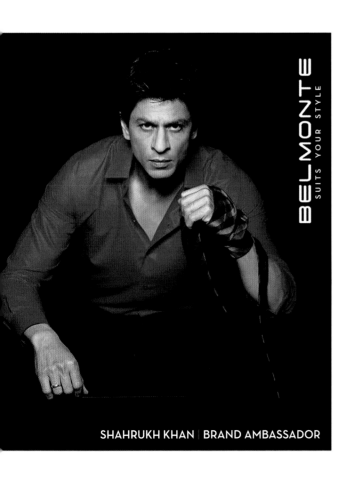

BELMONTE
SUITS YOUR STYLE

SHAHRUKH KHAN | BRAND AMBASSADOR

Tamarind
the flavour you wear

SHAMBHU KUMAR & NITIN KASLIWAL WITH HRITHIK ROSHAN
LAUNCH OF TAMARIIND | THE FLAVOUR YOU WEAR

SHAMBHU KUMAR & RAJKUMARI | MAHESHWAR HYDEL PROJECT

VIKAS RAPPELLING | LANDMARC CITI | MUMBAI

VIKAS KASLIWAL GO-KARTING | LANDMARC CITI | MUMBAI

INDOOR CRICKET | LANDMARC CITI | MUMBAI

VIKAS WITH TEAM LAGAAN | OSCAR PARTY | SHREE RAM MILLS PREMISES

VIDHI KASLIWAL WITH RAMAN LAMBA | INDOOR GOLF | LANDMARC CITI | MUMBAI

VINTAGE CAR EXHIBITION | SHREE RAM MILLS PREMISES

aspirational status immediately, and was adopted quickly by the rich and famous. By 2006, it was one of the flagship brands in the country. In its own way, Reid & Taylor changed the history of textiles in India, starting a trend that other companies would follow much later.

S.Kumars in due course would sign on Amitabh Bachchan as the style ambassador for Reid & Taylor; increasing its potential to appeal to a growing circle of buyers.

Nitin was also in the forefront of launching a series of labels, each with a celebrity vouching for its wearability. 'Tamariind,' renamed 'Cinnamon,' offered ready-made shirts that were modelled for the ads by Hrithik Roshan, while Shah Rukh Khan was the chosen ambassador for a line of fancy suitings

called 'Bellmonte.' India's first ever Miss Universe, Sushmita Sen, was signed for 'Carmichael House,' a household linen brand. As Nitin said in a press meet, 'We are clothiers to the nation today and will be to the world tomorrow.'

Under Ambuj's supervision, the Group also started an affordable department store called 'S-maart' which would provide all household essentials under one roof.

With encouragement from his father, Vikas started 'Landmarc Leisure Corporation Limited' that set up leisure centres in the heart of Mumbai and Indore. 'Landmarc Citi' was an Entertainment Theme Park with go-karting, amusement rides and food courts that had crowds flocking to it.

Seeing that he had set his nephews and sons on their individual paths to self-reliance in their chosen industries, in 2006, Shambhu Kumar divided the assets of the Group among them. He would retain the core textile business, concentrating on the diverse workwear materials created by S.Kumars. He continues to enjoy leadership in the uniforms market. ⑮

FRIEND, PHILOSOPHER AND GUIDE:
A Son's Point Of View

'That's what he has always been to me, a bit of all three; friend, philosopher and guide,' says Vikas Kasliwal, Shambhu Kumar's eldest son. Adding, 'I have never, since my early childhood, ever hesitated to say anything to him. And he has never discouraged me from bringing any issue to him. He has always seen my point of view. The best part is, he is never judgemental.'

Vikas remembers that there was an occasion when, perhaps for the very first time in his career as a student, he did not top the class. 'I fared poorly in my Intermediate exams,' he said, 'and my dad was curious about why it had happened. I spoke to him, confessed that my flying lessons and new friendships had distracted me. He listened carefully, and all he said was, "It's okay. You need to see the downs too." He always senses my failures and gives me advice that is constructive.'

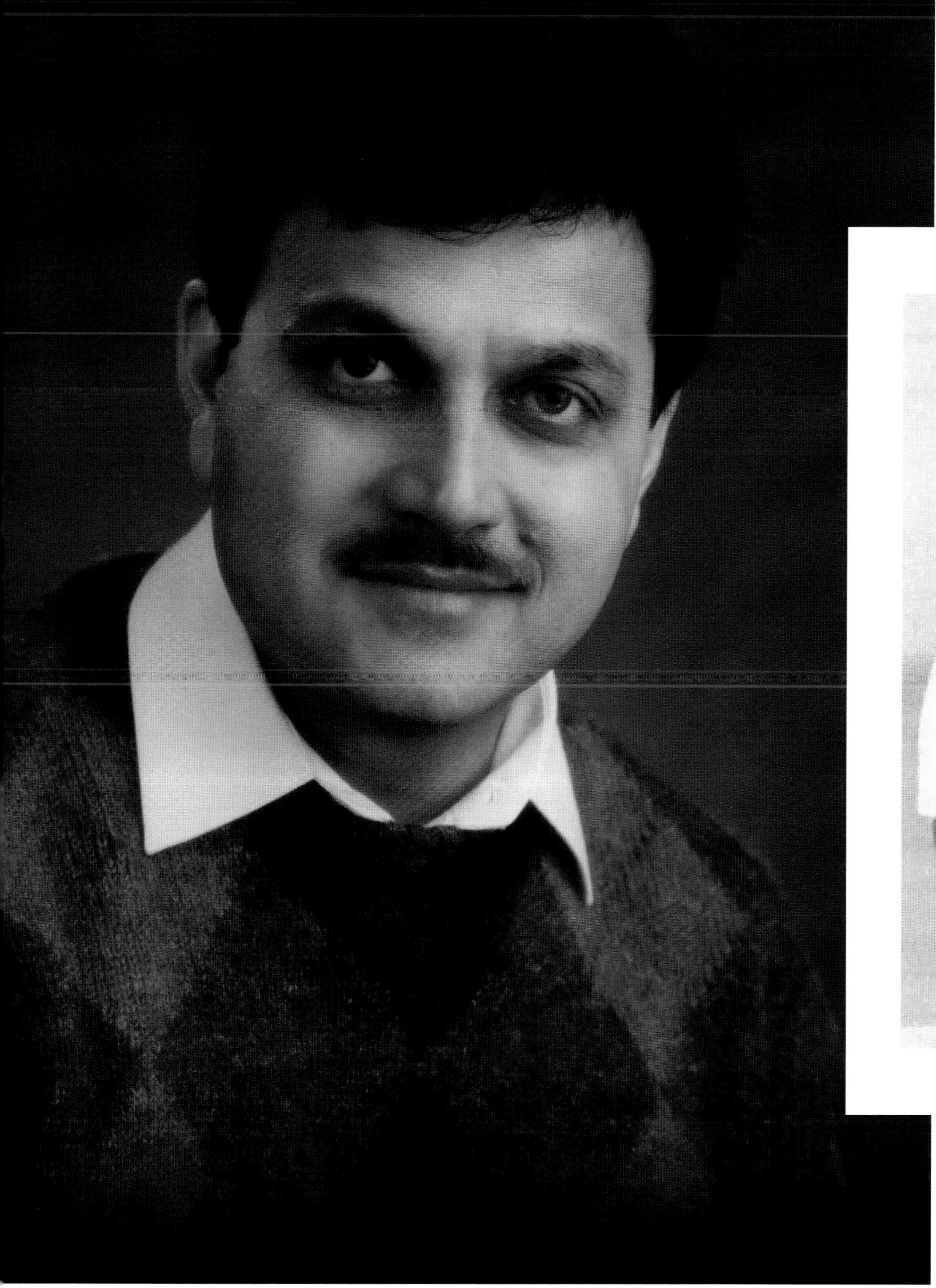

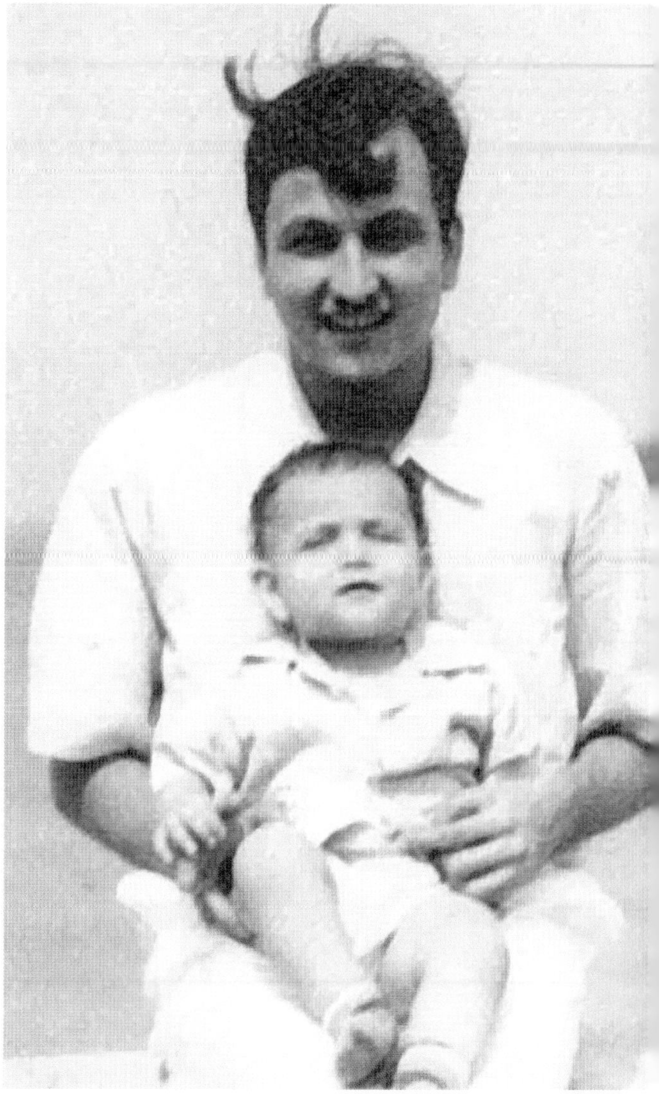

WITH PARENTS

WITH WIFE ANURADHA & CHILDREN

Vikas remembers the time he was spearheading the association with Michelin Tyres as part of the Group's expansion plans. 'The French tie-up was hugely prestigious. But things went awry when Roger Mora, who was key to our negotiations with Michelin, suddenly expired. The entire collaboration fell apart, I felt a complete failure. But my father stood solidly by me.

He supported me, advising me as a friend would. Of course, we benefited financially as we got huge damages from Michelin, but for me it was a personal failure. I had wanted to build the brand, bringing in a steady and lasting source of income.'

Vikas admires his father's ability to distinguish between theoretical morals

and practical morals. 'He is wise to the ways of the world and advises us to be aware of this difference in moral stances,' he says, adding that theoretical morals is what appears to be right or wrong in theory, while practical morals is what in reality is right or wrong. 'The difference, my father pointed out to us, is whether there is an intention to harm.'

WITH PARENTS & SIBLINGS

FAMILY VACATION | NEW ZEALAND | 2007

VIKAS KASLIWAL, WITH HIS FATHER'S BLESSINGS, EMBARKED ON DEVELOPING THE PALAIS ROYALE PROJECT IN MUMBAI, WHICH WOULD BOAST OF BEING THE TALLEST RESIDENTIAL BUILDING IN INDIA WITH THE HIGHEST ATRIUM AND DEEPEST TRANSFER GIRDER IN THE WORLD.

Elaborating on this thought, Vikas explains how his father would tell them about handling competition and influence in society and business. 'My father's view is, "You have to swim in the pond, follow the rules in the same pond … so you have to find ways to help yourself. This is fine as long as you do not hurt anyone in the process, or influence anyone to deliver hurt. It is fine to promote yourself, but not by obstructing another. And do not indulge in any kind of activities where you make money selling sub-standard stuff, or by cheating. Give the right material at competitive prices, business will thrive." He always taught us by example, and adhered to his principles throughout,' Vikas adds.

One of Shambhu Kumar's favourite sayings is also his son's favourite. 'Every saint has a past, and every sinner a future,' he truly believes. And that when destiny throws a spanner

in the works, one must do one's best to get around the problem, "*Munh mein Ram, pag par dhyan*." 'My father lived by this in his days of ill health,' Vikas says. 'He was terribly unwell, but did not give up,' for him it was important to pass the day. Vikas also credits his father for always 'doing the right thing.'

'I do believe I am considered to be his "favourite," but he has always been a fair father and never gone all out or all against any of us to take sides. However, it is true that my father has always taken care of my needs, even more than my mother,' Vikas adds. 'When I was in school, knowing my craze for books and reading, he indulged me by buying me entire sets of knowledge books. I was even allowed to get the Encyclopaedia Britannica.

'Again, when I was leaving for Harvard, in 1977 when the foreign exchange rules were stringent about carrying foreign currency, he made me carry a gold chain and bracelet, telling me they were my safety net. I could easily convert them to cash anytime or in an emergency.'

His father's attitude towards his children has influenced his own as a father to his, according to Vikas. 'I have learnt to give space to my children; allow them to make mistakes and just be a safety net. I learnt how important it is to let a child know that you are always there,' he says.

Vikas also has a deep admiration for the filial duties his father has carried out towards his own father and his wife. 'His father, my grandfather, was a very nice man. He was always there for my father, even though he did not leave any material inheritance for him. With the children from my grandfather's third marriage, it was a one-way relationship. My father took care of all of them, accepting them as his responsibility with equanimity, and treating his step-mother with all the deference and respect he would have given his own mother. In that he was superlative.

'My dad is a true karma yogi,' Vikas says. 'He has always carried along all those above and below him. And he has done this without any fear or favour and without any desire for the fruit.' ⑤

FATHER & SON | SIGNING
THE MICHELIN DEAL

HE IS AN ABSOLUTE ROCKSTAR: A Son's Tribute

'I started working with my dad when I was 16. I had finished my 12th and joined science, with the aim of getting into medicine,' says Nitin Kasliwal, Shambhu Kumar's second son. 'But my father asked, "what will you do, BSc *ke baad*..." and roped me into textiles. I would attend morning classes from 7 to 10 at Jai Hind College, in South Bombay and then go to our first process house at Andheri by train.'

Somehow his father sensed Nitin would be more inclined towards textiles than the others, so 'he directed me to train for six months, to begin with. He put me through the entire grind, making me start at the very bottom and work my way up.' Nitin feels very grateful for this, because 'my entire understanding of the textile line came to me thanks to it. All aspects of manufacturing, processing, marketing, finance, purchase ... I came to know every facet of the business quite thoroughly.'

WITH FATHER S.KUMARS DEALER MEET

WITH WIFE JYOTI, CHILDREN & PARENTS

Shambhu Kumar's idea of making his son start at the shop floor was so he could get acquainted with the staff at that level. 'It would "keep my feet on the ground," so to say. So, there I was working shoulder to shoulder with workers, and the factory manager was my boss. It was great training for a 16-year-old, not just in the business aspects, but in human relations.'

Nitin remembers thoroughly enjoying himself as he worked with the team,

'and got fully immersed. Of course, my studies went for a complete toss. I had been a distinction student till the 12th, but now, college took second place as I was busy getting practical education and training. I have no regrets, though I had dreamt of doing my MBA, which did not happen then as I was in the thick of business.'

Of course, that got remedied later. 'When I was 30, in 1990, I took a sabbatical and completed my

THE FOUR SIBLINGS

FAMILY VACATION SWITZERLAND 2005

Masters in Business Administration from Switzerland. It was 14 years after I had got into the business. I was married and had two kids by then. But Jyoti, my wife, and my father worked it all out so I could complete my degree.'

Nitin believes that his father and he are very close and alike in many ways; not just genetically. 'He has a large heart, and a strong grasp on things; intuitively he understands a situation or a process, and 'I humbly say that these are qualities I share with him. I picked them up inherently and practically, working so closely with him.

'Ours was a family-run business, with my father being hands-on. He knew exactly what was happening with his dealers, agents, and how the sales were going. We were the only textile company in the country to have an all-India dealer network penetrating into the rural and interior parts of the country. And this was the backbone of our business.'

Nitin was amazed at his father's endearing relationship with his dealers. 'They loved him, and would give their lives for us. This is a rare thing in business. The trust factor was very high; my father never exploited the dealers, rather, he went out of his way and helped when he could. I learnt that from him. I think this is something we all learnt from him ... fairness and honesty in business ... and fearlessness.'

Having pleasant memories of the long car rides they took together as a family, Nitin says, 'My father was quite the maverick, he was never afraid of driving with the entire family, even if it was midnight. And he took risks in business that many would have baulked at. We are thankful to him for teaching us not to be afraid of anyone, and to always be honest.

'Of course, we all enjoyed a lot of success, but his view was, "okay, now this is done, *aage ka soocho*," and he would look for a new goal.

"Dream big, but stay grounded; make mistakes, but learn from them; treat every person well, even if they are economically weaker than you": are some of his father's teachings that resonate with Nitin even today. 'My dad says, "You can achieve whatever you want to achieve but keep your heart clean. Trust in God and have faith in yourself." He says, "Do not wish harm to anybody; then even if things go wrong, God will stand by you, you will come out of your troubles." It's advice that has stood me in good stead.'

As far back as Nitin can remember, his father has been a workaholic. 'His entire life revolved around work. Of course, I realise now that he had to work hard, he was supporting his family and his father's family; almost 25-30 of us in all. But at that time, I wondered why he was so inaccessible; always busy. My mom was the anchor who looked after us and the home. She was my conduit to my dad.

'My father is a Rockstar. Very few people are able to build a business from scratch with absolutely nothing. People were, and are, in awe of him. Even so, he has always been humble. To me he is an absolute Rockstar, my role model. ⑤

WITH DELEGATES | DEWAS | 1995

EDUCATED, UNEDUCATED PARENTS: A Son Speaks

'As the third son, and the youngest in the family for all of seven years, till sister Neerja was born, I was pampered by all,' says Mukul Kasliwal. 'In fact, as we lived in a joint family set-up, and if you count the cousins, I had four, not two, brothers older than me. It made being the youngest all the more advantageous.'

Mukul's memories of his childhood are more closely linked to his mother, Rajkumari, who would take him along on the trips to the South, necessitated by the Group's link-up with Madura Coats. He remembers the many dealers who would consider themselves part of the S.Kumars family and endeavour to make his day special. 'Narendra Chettiyar or Bushy uncle, so named by me, as he had a dog by that name, would take me to Guindy Park in Madras. We often stayed at Woodlands Hotel, and someone there would take me and buy me the typical Rasiklal supari. These remain pleasant memories of my childhood,' he adds. Trips to Marina Beach, to Tirupati with Bhau Saheb Apte and his parents, where 'Bhau Saheb

would carry me on his shoulders through the queues to the sanctum sanctorum calling out to Govinda the Lord of Tirumalai, all the way,' are other happy memories that Mukul recollects.

'We had a Grundig turntable. My father loved listening to "Que Sera, Sera," "Ya Mustafa," and "Summer Wine," among others. In that sense ours was a non-conservative family.' Unlike his siblings who studied at Villa Theresa on Peddar Road, Mukul attended the Breach Candy Primary school on the adjoining Warden Road in Bombay, for by then Villa Theresa had stopped taking boys.

He remembers himself as a chubby kid; 'I loved eating chips,' and a bit of a 'mother's boy,' spending more time with her. And that he was sensitive (something his mother says he still is). 'I had a hyper-sensitive nature,' Mukul says, 'I would go and stand in the balcony and pout and sulk, despite the fact that my older siblings, brothers and cousins all showered me with affection.'

Mukul was, as the youngest child, 'growing up with a sense of entitlement. I would do mostly what I wanted. Drink Coke and get a sugar rush and dance ... ' but he also remembers a sobering moment 'when my father slapped me. He was always strict, and had a quick, hot temper to match; in fact, I am more like my father in nature.'

When Mukul was awarded his Honours Degree at Greenwich, he paid tribute to his parents. 'I dedicated my acceptance speech to "My educated, uneducated parents,"' he says. 'Of course, they both attended my convocation. To them, my being recognised was as significant as it was for me.'

He credits his father for grounding in him and his siblings a sense of responsibility. 'It made me want to act in a manner that would make my parents proud.' He mentions an example during a train trip to Nepal with the other students of the St. Xavier's Boys' Academy. 'We would stay on the platform every night. My father had let me go alone, of course, but he had

A YOUNG MUKUL WITH PARENTS

BROTHERS & SISTER INDORE 1973

WITH BHAU SAHEB APTE

WITH WIFE URAVI & FAMILY ON VACATION CHINA 2006

MUKUL KASLIWAL, BACKED BY THE TEACHINGS OF HIS FATHER, TOGETHER WITH COUSIN WARIJ, ACQUIRED KLOPMAN INTERNATIONAL, A WORLD-RENOWNED MANUFACTURER OF PROTECTIVE, CORPORATE AND CASUAL APPAREL AND WORKWEAR, WITH ITS HEADQUARTERS IN FROSINONE, ITALY.

L TO R | AMBUJ KASLIWAL, BAIRAM VAKIL, SHIRISH DALAL, MUKUL KASLIWAL, VIJAY KALANTRI, ANAND RATHI, S.P. BANERJEE, G.P. SINGH, VIKAS KASLIWAL & ANIRUDDH KASLIWAL | MUMBAI | 2000

make money without cheating, or stealing that which belongs to others ... something almost unheard of in business today. 'But I have watched my father manage to steer the company to great heights without taking recourse to such practices.

'I have seen success and power and what it does to people, and I have seen my parents, and how different they are. They remain unchanged through highs and lows, and their ability to sacrifice is supreme. Their happiness is always placed after ours. And I have seen how, time after time, they maintain their integrity and courage when they have to face challenges.'

To Mukul, S.Kumars is, 'A Name you can Trust,' and a company that has always been ahead of its time, holding close, values that no one can change. ◉

given me the telephone numbers of the dealers and friends all along the way, at every station, in case I should need any help.

'On the way back from Nepal, the train was running quite late. I felt my parents would be worried. So, I went to the Railway Post Office and sent a telegram informing them of the delay. I felt it was my responsibility to let them know, so they would not worry. None of the other boys did anything similar,' he adds, 'but my father's teaching ran deep. Keeping the communication lines with family open constantly, is important for him, and thus, for me.

Even during my honeymoon, I would stay in touch, calling twice a day. And in turn, I have taught the same sense of responsibility to my son.'

Mukul believes it is this training that has stood by him, making him take up every challenge in business head on, and seeing it through. And he feels it is important to

WITH HIS MOM

NEERJA BIRLA

EVERY PRINCIPLE OF LIFE I HAVE LEARNT IS FROM THEM:
A Daughter's Love

Marriage into one of the country's biggest industry houses has not cut the links Neerja Birla, Shambhu Kumar and Rajkumari's only daughter, has with her parents and siblings. 'Now more than ever, I am in constant touch with my mom and dad,' she says adding, 'when I was young, he was just too, too busy. Being a first generation entrepreneur, he had to carve his own path, fight his own battles and grow despite any odds that he faced. So, it was my mother whom we were with most of the time, concerning school and studies and all aspects of growing up. Though we did go to Kashmir and Mount Abu for holidays where the family was close together.'

Being the 'baby' of the family, Neerja was doted on by everyone, especially Abhay Kumar and his wife. Neerja had a very special bond with 'Pappa.' He had named her and named the home they built in Indore after her. Whenever they would go to Neerja Villa, the little girl would spend her time idyllically cycling, playing table tennis, carrom and drinking pineapple-flavoured Energy Milk which had been carried along from Bombay.

Neerja says she has imbibed from her father the huge learning of not taking life too seriously. 'He taught us to laugh at ourselves. I would get angry and say, "You don't understand how difficult it is for me," about some issue, and he would laugh … it has helped me navigate through all the challenges I have met.'

In his typical way, Shambhu Kumar did not differentiate between his children. 'He brought me up as an equal to my brothers. In fact, it was my overprotective brothers, rather than my father, who tried to quell my rather unbridled spirit of adventure. My father's never-say-die attitude has been the fulcrum of my life.'

Neerja sees in her father, 'a hardworking man, who created an exceptional company on the B-to-B model and kept it growing through his relationship with dealers. He was always one-on-one, with amazing people skills,' she adds. 'Also notable is his integrity and his clean and above-board way of handling his business. And it showed in everything, including his life as a Rotarian.' She remembers how once, while in Ooty, it was pouring and they were unable to find the location of the Rotary Club meeting, but her father would not give up and finally made it.

Neerja finds her commitments do come in the way of her time with her parents. Recently, 'We went to Mahabaleshwar for three or four days … Even now, it is not easy to tear him away from work.' A trip they made together to Austria is one of her most enduring and joyful memories.

BABY NEERJA WITH ABHAY KUMAR

WITH HUSBAND KUMARMANGALAM & CHILDREN

NEERJA WITH HER FIVE BROTHERS

FAMILY VACATION | AUSTRIA | 2013

Though the 'standing joke and the bone of contention' in the family is that Vikas 'Dada' is her father's favourite, and it is to Vikas he turns when he is not well, when he is emotional and wants to talk, 'it is me he calls,' she says. 'Like parents of all daughters, I think my mom and dad too feel they should not have married me off so young, they feel they should have kept me with them for some years more.' Neerja was engaged at 16, and married when she turned 18.

And what a grand affair it was. A huge matter of joy for everyone and the entire family participated in making the wedding a warm spectacle. An inclusive and systematic way was worked out as every Marwari ceremony had to be held correctly and perfectly.

The four main functions were divided among the four wives of the four married brothers; thus, each was given a responsibility. It was in some ways, an extension of how Shambhu Kumar conducted his enterprise. There was a sit down lunch for over 700 *baraatis* that filled all the banquet rooms of the Taj Mahal Palace in Bombay and the service was done, not by the waiters, but by the entire Kasliwal tribe that included the family members, the S.Kumars staff, agents, dealers, et al.

Flashback to her school days, Neerja remembers an early lesson. 'I had somebody else's eraser in my compass box. My mother asked me about it, I casually replied it wasn't mine. She was livid, and slapped me. My father reiterated, "Never take what does not belong to you." I have never forgotten that lesson.'

Of her parents she says, they have no inkling of space, they are so close that they are as good as one person. 'I have never seen them fight, or have an argument. Today of course they argue, as my mother worries over his health, and he can be defiant and careless about taking unnecessary risks. But except for the rare occasions she might have gone with us to see a movie without him, I doubt my parents have even spent a single night apart from each other. She goes everywhere he goes, including to both offices at extreme ends of the city.

'But now I see the equation as somewhat changed. Earlier he led, she followed, but now he lets her take the decisions. At home, mother has always been in charge. And now elsewhere too.' Shambhu Kumar relies on Rajkumari to be his eyes and ears, and memory card too.

'I'm blessed to have such parents,' she adds. 'Every principle of life I have learnt from them, is valuable and guides me even today.' ◉

WITH HER DAD

LOOKING TO THE FUTURE

Both Dhvani and Vidhi, who are Vikas' daughters, enjoy a special relationship with their grandparents. Their earliest joyful memories are of the times spent with Shambhu Kumar and Rajkumari ... 'This was always Dadi's house for me,' Dhvani says. 'Thanks to the shared kitchen, we came here for lunch and dinner. We have happy memories of meal times, of being spoilt silly by Dadi.'

'On weekends we would stay with our grandparents; it was something that both Dhvani and I, as well as our grandparents so looked forward to,' adds Vidhi. 'They had a fold-out bed in their room, and we would sleep there.'

The children loved being 'really spoilt.'

Rajkumari bonded with Vidhi over the fact that they are both foodies. 'Mom was strict about not eating Peppy, and chips and all that she termed as junk food; Milan supari, Fatafat, were other things out of bounds for us at home. But knowing how much I enjoyed these, Dadi would get them for me.' Dhvani remembers her favourite foods, courtesy her grandmother: *mutter paratha*, onion pancake, chilli cheese toast ... 'Ask for anything and she would somehow get it. Dadi would manage it even if there was no kitchen help.'

The girls fondly remember their 'desks in Dadi's house, where we would sit and do our homework. Then play make-believe games and eventually have our meals together, retiring to our flat only when it was bedtime. Earlier it was on a different floor so we had to take the lift; now of course our houses are on the same floor.'

'In the old set-up, they had a TV set; and a sofa on which we would sit and watch for hours on end.' 'Chitrahaar,' 'BPL Top 20,' and the game shows were favourite programmes watched to the steady crunching of chips dipped in salsa. 'I would sit *ulta* and watch,' Vidhi says laughing.

Of their granddad, both girls have somewhat distinct views. 'Vidhi was obviously his favourite,' Dhvani remarks, and Vidhi counters that 'Dhvani was Mom's. Though they treated us both equally.'

Dhvani says of her grandfather that she loved his way of making everything humorous. 'He was not the typical grandfather; too busy to interact with his grandchildren, sitting with a newspaper and his spectacles on his nose. Rather, he brought humour into everything. And taught us so much with his sayings; he was always spouting proverbs in all languages, including Marathi, Gujarati, Sanskrit, English and Marwari. "Stretch your legs

only as much as your sheet can cover," was one of his favourites,' she adds.

'Also, he was extremely busy, but we would interact during the pilgrimage tours or the long drives we took together. Today my children say, "how boring," when I talk about these trips, but we had a load of fun, our music playing in the car, full volume, Cheese Balls and Peppy and us two sisters lying down in the back seat as we drove at full speed, often all the way to Indore from Bombay.'

Vidhi recollects a trip they took to Agra, Mount Abu, Chittor and other parts of Rajasthan. 'The drivers would struggle to follow in another car, as Dadi cruised along at 100 per hour. Daddu would be insistent we note the towns as we passed them, the mileage we made ... though at that time we would wonder why, it was education of a different, informal kind, but every bit as valuable.'

Rajkumari would drive the children to school, 'if the driver did not turn up.'

Vidhi remembers waiting eagerly for her dad and grandpa to come back from work, 'and us eating together. They would continue to talk shop, and I would eavesdrop on these work discussions. Although I wouldn't really follow everything being

said, it fascinated me and probably ignited an ambition in me. As it happens, my dad continues to ask his father for advice; though the relationship has changed; they are now more like friends. They still have their morning tea together; and meet after dinner. If my father is late any day, Dadi will call to check if he's okay.' Vidhi adds that her father has always been an obedient son. 'He had made it clear that he would marry someone his parents chose for him. My mother in turn, has a lot of respect for my grandparents; she knows how much they have done for the family, and continue to do even today,' she adds. 'My mom is hot-headed, and my dadi is cool. Their personalities are diverse, but looking at them, one can learn a lot about how to beautifully compromise to keep up relationships. There's never been a harsh word about my grandparents from Mom; unlike in many families where a mother feels insecure about the in-laws' relationship with her children and influences them against the older people. That does not exist in our family.'

Dhvani shares a story about her marriage that speaks volumes of her grandparents' approach to life and relationships. 'I was in a long, secret relationship for six years,' she says. 'Dadi knew, in fact all knew about it. He would drop me outside and drive off. Dadi would say, "Tell him to drop you inside as it is late." We had pretty strict deadlines for coming home, so often Vidhi would be with me, and we would return by 11 pm. Then after a point of observing all this, Dadi announced it was high time we got married. In fact, we had been stalling as he had to go overseas, but now things came to a head. We did get married and fly to Washington DC for two years. Dadi would keep saying it was the right thing to do; Vidhi's would happen in due course, when she's ready.'

Working in the S.Kumars business came to the two granddaughters differently, at different times. Dhvani started working five years after her second child. 'I'd go to the S.Kumars office and spend a few hours with Daddu. As I became more mature, I understood the importance of being part of his organisation. S.Kumars, I realised, was a huge brand name, and being the third generation which as the saying goes, is responsible for a brand starting to crumble, I felt I should ensure I do whatever possible to prevent that from happening. I had till then, only eaten the fruit of the tree. I needed to nourish and revitalise the tree itself. Daddu had broken his back to make the brand; we had to keep the flag flying.'

Dhvani mentions an example of the respect the S.Kumars name evoked. 'We would go to a restaurant for dinner; and be told it was full and we needed to wait outside. While noting our name for calling out, they would see "Kasliwal" and immediately usher us to the best table that was reserved for unexpected VIP customers.'

Dhvani took up serious duties in the company, when four years ago, her cousin

SHAMBHU KUMAR ENDOWING GRANDDAUGHTER DHVANI

Utkarsh, Warij's son, who had been working with Shambhu Kumar for eight years, could no longer continue, due to unavoidable circumstances.

Dhvani says, 'I was enjoying what I was doing in the office; my curiosity had made me dip my fingers into the workings of all sections. I understood it well. Vidhi was far away from all this, making award-winning films; and when Utkarsh stopped coming, I was the only one left.' Her early duties had included checking on tenders, companies, part of the "Institutional Department," which was a very niche assignment to begin with. 'I started from zero but listened closely to Daddu, and learnt quickly,' Dhvani says. 'Later, I was given finance to handle.'

Dhvani might just as well have joined her own father-in-law's fabrication company, except for the fact that she wanted to be a teacher once the children grew up. 'I even started at a small school, but ended up taking on S.Kumars' duties. The company was heading towards 75 years of a fruitful existence, I saw tremendous possibilities for us to explore.'

Dhvani worked with the staff very diplomatically, keeping open channels of communicating with them. 'I am also very hard-working and seeing how I was putting in a lot of effort to contribute in my own way to theirs, the team began to accept me.' By following her grandfather's example of treating everyone respectfully and speaking as an equal with them all, she earned her staffers' respect. 'It's been six years since I joined, and now Vidhi and I have full responsibility,' she adds. 'My duties are in Marketing and Finance.'

Her day begins with dropping the kids off to school and then spending from 10.30 to 3.30 in office. 'I have to be quick,' she says. 'It's back-to-back; I have so much to do, to cram into a short day.' Her time, she explains, is hectic both at work and at home, with a daughter who is 11 and a son at 13. 'It's dealing with their emotional ups and downs and their homework and everything in between. Sometimes I work at night, or in the park; in fact whenever I can snatch extra time. I feel I must complete my tasks, it is a Big Responsibility. I spend Saturdays with the kids and keep Saturday nights for any work I might have brought home. I only take morning-evening trips, when I have to. Because I keep in mind what my grandfather has told me, that the family comes first.'

Vidhi traces her journey into the Group. 'Daddu had already started training Dhvani. The company was going through trying years at that time due to the pandemic. Papa could sense Daddu's innate desire that I should join textiles.

'Papa put the germ in my mind, but I kept shooting the idea down; it was not my passion. The lockdown gave us all many opportunities and a lot of time for both discussion and introspection, and I thought to myself, maybe it's time to grow up. Daddu insisted, "don't let your passion die," and encouraged me to keep it alive even as I started learning the ropes of the production end of the business, splitting my time between Mumbai and Indore.

'My days are different, depending on where I am. When in Indore, I am at the factory in Dewas, five days at

SHAMBHU KUMAR BLESSING GRANDDAUGHTER VIDHI

DHVANI WITH HUSBAND & CHILDREN

AT WORK | S.KUMARS OFFICE | NIRANJAN

WITH HER DADDU

WITH HER DADI

VIDHI BEHIND THE CAMERA

INSPECTING OUTPUT | S.KUMARS FACTORY | DEWAS

WITH HER DADI

THE TWO SISTERS

WITH HER DADDU

SHAMBHU KUMAR & HIS FAMILY

AFTER YOU PASS MANY YEARS, AGE IS JUST A NUMBER. YOU ARE AS OLD OR AS YOUNG AS YOU FEEL IN YOUR MIND. I AM STILL YOUNG, AT THE AGE OF 92 I SAY I STILL LEARN HOW THE WORLD TURNS.

– SHAMBHU KUMAR

a stretch. I meet with different departments, on fixed days of the week, to take updates and understand and solve their difficulties ... they have been doing their work for so long, I only need to oversee. And plan strategy to expand production. I marvel at how well they have accepted me; I did have apprehensions about this, but it's worked out well. What's more is, it's fun to work with Dhvani. I look up to how diligently she carries out her role.'

Vidhi adds, 'We sisters felt we owed it to Daddu, who along with Bade Dada ji had built this huge edifice with respect and integrity, literally from rags to riches, which then our Kakas and Papa strengthened. And lo and behold! To my surprise, I started enjoying it. It gives me structure and discipline. Earlier, I used to produce films and now I'm going to produce cloth too!

'Of course, our grandfather tells us to think before we act, keep things consolidated, and to take everything step by step. He has always told us, "Never be afraid of hardships, risks or failures," as he has also used that mantra for himself,' Vidhi sums it up. 'His favourite song is "*Tadbeer se bigdi hui taqdeer bana le*" and he particularly likes the line, "*Haari hui baahon ko hi patwaar bana le, apne pe bharosa hai to yeh daav laga le*" ... '

Perhaps Vidhi and Dhvani are the *patwaars* he is trusting now.

Indeed, as always, Shambhu Kumar seems to have made the right move. Perhaps he will recreate the 'winning combination' he had with his elder brother, in this partnership with his granddaughters. Today, with the force of an untiring team behind them, the two granddaughters have managed to turn the early scepticism of those within and outside the family into admiration. Their steady focus is on keeping the uniform section, which remains the company's flag-bearer division, running side-by-side with their grandmother's towelling unit, productive and profitable. Like the example set for them, they continue the brand's tradition of integrity and high value goods at affordable, competitive rates.

Shambhu Kumar, of course, is watching, guiding, his hand on the rudder as his granddaughters drive the company to its next port of success. With the S.Kumars flag flying merrily in the winds of the future. ⓢ

THE *S.Kumars* JOURNEY

1950s

Agency of **Ellichpur Cotton Mills** near Nagpur

Agency of **Kohinoor Mills**, Bombay

Promoted & Popularised **Synthetic Cloth**

S.Kumars Logo designed by Nishikant Shirodkar

Younger brother **Sumati Kumar** joined the business

1970s

Agency of **Laxmi Vishnu Mills**, Solapur: **Terene, Voiles, Poplins**

Launched Terene saris: **S.Kumar ki Sariyan**

Sponsored Chat Show on Radio **Aap aur Hum**

Sponsored Radio Show **Mukkadama** with Dicky Rutnagar interviewing Star Cricketers

Sumati Kumar shifted back to Indore, branched out into **Real Estate**

Ambuj (son of Abhay Kumar) involved in Sales of Textiles

Sponsored Radio Show with Ameen Sayani interviewing Film Personalities: **S.Kumar ka Filmi Mukkadama**

Shambhu Kumar turned **Industrialist**: Took Dilkhush Dyeing & turned it into **SKM Fabrics** Processing House, Andheri, Bombay

Warij (son of Abhay Kumar) involved in Production of Diversified Industrial Rubber Products at newly obtained **Modak Rubber Products** in Bombay

Opened a packing centre, **S.Kumar House** in Marol, Bombay

Acquired **Shree Ram Mills** (Spinning to Processing): **Super-fine, High-value Cotton Fabrics: Rubia, Voiles, Dhotis, Tracing Fabric**

Vikas (son of Shambhu Kumar) involved in full-fledged Production of Textiles

Laid foundation of **SKM Amana** Processing Mill at Dewas

Expanded the Nation-wide network of **Semi-Wholesalers** all over India

Began **Fashion Shows** choreographed by Shanti Chopra at **Dealer Conferences**

Introduced **Polyacron** a unique blend of Polyester, Acrylic & Viscose

Tied up with **Ahmed Woollen Mills**, Thana: Forayed into **Light-weight Woollens**

Formulated **Incentive Schemes** for **Dealers & Retailers**

Organised the **Retailer Gift Unit Scheme**, direct contact with over 35,000 Retailers all over India

Janmashtami 1948
Shambhu Kumar created S.Kumars

Purchased & Sold Cloth in the **Mulji Jetha Market**
Older brother **Abhay Kumar** joined the business

1948

1960s

Secured exclusive deal between **ICI (Imperial Chemical Industries)** & Kohinoor Mills for **Terylene**

Pioneered all types of **Blends & Finishes: Polyester Cotton (PC), Polyester Viscose (PV), Gabardine, Matte**

Emergence of the **S.Kumars Uniforms Business**

Agency of **Shree Ram Silks**, Rishra near Calcutta; **Ramesh Silk Mills**, Surat; **Madura Mills (Madura Coats)**, Ambasamudram near Madurai

Sole Selling Agency of **Export Surplus** of **CAFI (Chemicals & Fibres of India)**: **Ready-made Shirts, Suitings, Crepe** Ladies-wear material

Established Nation-wide network of **Wholesalers** all over India

Commenced **Prompt Payment Discounts (PPD)**

Instituted the **SK Foundation (Charitable) Trust**

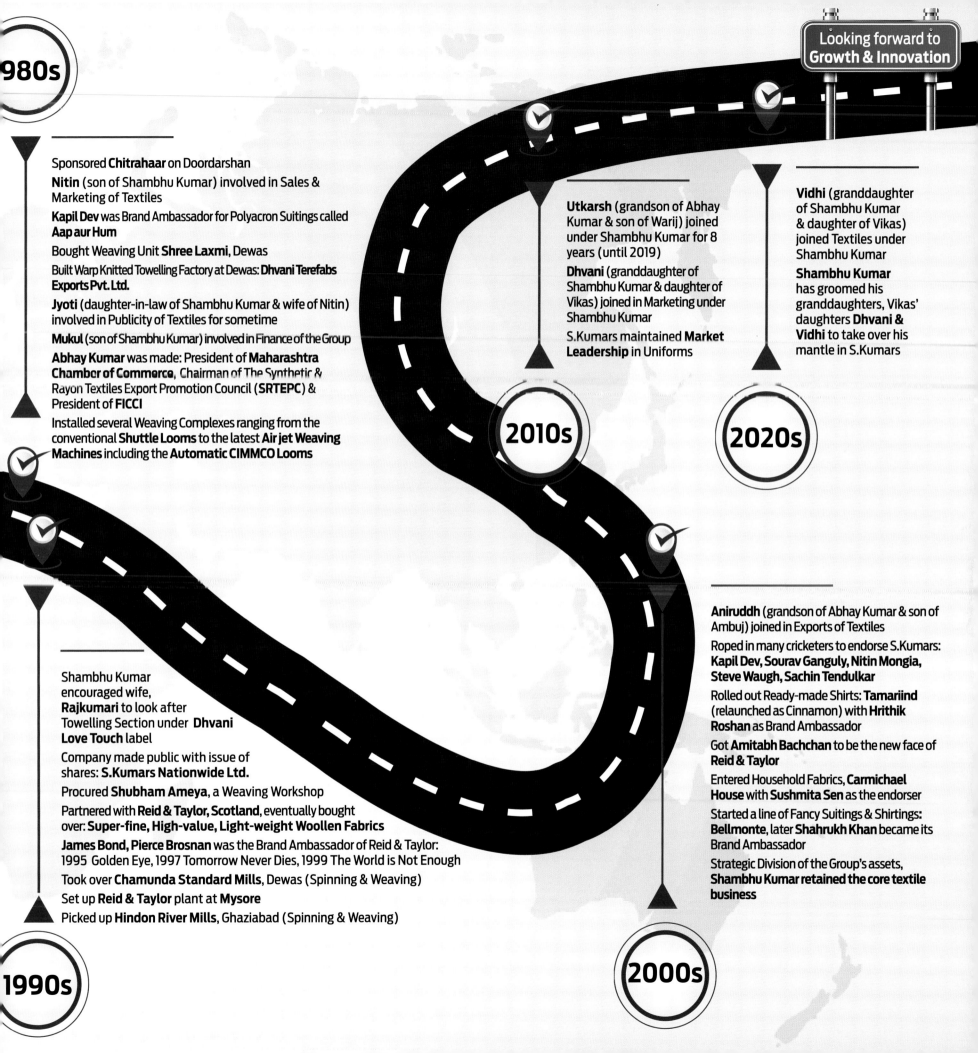

980s

Sponsored **Chitrahaar** on Doordarshan

Nitin (son of Shambhu Kumar) involved in Sales & Marketing of Textiles

Kapil Dev was Brand Ambassador for Polyacron Suitings called **Aap aur Hum**

Bought Weaving Unit **Shree Laxmi**, Dewas

Built Warp Knitted Towelling Factory at Dewas: **Dhvani Terefabs Exports Pvt. Ltd.**

Jyoti (daughter-in-law of Shambhu Kumar & wife of Nitin) involved in Publicity of Textiles for sometime

Mukul (son of Shambhu Kumar) involved in Finance of the Group

Abhay Kumar was made: President of **Maharashtra Chamber of Commerce**, Chairman of The Synthetic & Rayon Textiles Export Promotion Council (**SRTEPC**) & President of **FICCI**

Installed several Weaving Complexes ranging from the conventional **Shuttle Looms** to the latest **Air jet Weaving Machines** including the **Automatic CIMMCO Looms**

Looking forward to Growth & Innovation

Utkarsh (grandson of Abhay Kumar & son of Warij) joined under Shambhu Kumar for 8 years (until 2019)

Dhvani (granddaughter of Shambhu Kumar & daughter of Vikas) joined in Marketing under Shambhu Kumar

S.Kumars maintained **Market Leadership** in Uniforms

2010s

Vidhi (granddaughter of Shambhu Kumar & daughter of Vikas) joined Textiles under Shambhu Kumar

Shambhu Kumar has groomed his granddaughters, Vikas' daughters **Dhvani & Vidhi** to take over his mantle in S.Kumars

2020s

Shambhu Kumar encouraged wife, **Rajkumari** to look after Towelling Section under **Dhvani Love Touch** label

Company made public with issue of shares: **S.Kumars Nationwide Ltd.**

Procured **Shubham Ameya**, a Weaving Workshop

Partnered with **Reid & Taylor, Scotland**, eventually bought over: **Super-fine, High-value, Light-weight Woollen Fabrics**

James Bond, Pierce Brosnan was the Brand Ambassador of Reid & Taylor: 1995 Golden Eye, 1997 Tomorrow Never Dies, 1999 The World is Not Enough

Took over **Chamunda Standard Mills**, Dewas (Spinning & Weaving)

Set up **Reid & Taylor** plant at **Mysore**

Picked up **Hindon River Mills**, Ghaziabad (Spinning & Weaving)

1990s

Aniruddh (grandson of Abhay Kumar & son of Ambuj) joined in Exports of Textiles

Roped in many cricketers to endorse S.Kumars: **Kapil Dev, Sourav Ganguly, Nitin Mongia, Steve Waugh, Sachin Tendulkar**

Rolled out Ready-made Shirts: **Tamariind** (relaunched as Cinnamon) with **Hrithik Roshan** as Brand Ambassador

Got **Amitabh Bachchan** to be the new face of **Reid & Taylor**

Entered Household Fabrics, **Carmichael House** with **Sushmita Sen** as the endorser

Started a line of Fancy Suitings & Shirtings: **Bellmonte**, later **Shahrukh Khan** became its Brand Ambassador

Strategic Division of the Group's assets, **Shambhu Kumar retained the core textile business**

2000s

S.Kumars®

The Fabric of India
Since 1948

ACKNOWLEDGEMENTS

With lists like these there are bound to be errors and omissions. We would like to apologise in advance for the names we might have missed. But their contribution has not been forgotten. We would like to recognise the role of each and every person who has helped make S.Kumars what it was, what it is and what it could be.

TRADE

Laxman Vaman 'Bhau Saheb' Apte & the entire Apte Family

Manorama 'Vahini' Apte | Manju & Kamlakar Modak | Kuma & Datta Rajwade | Madhav Rao & Sheela Apte | Arvind Rao & Suniti Apte

Ajay S. Shriram (Delhi Cloth Mills, Ghaziabad)
Allied Textiles PLC, UK (Reid & Taylor, Scotland)
Arun Bajoria (CIMMCO Looms)
Bangurs (Shree Ram Silks, Rishra)
Bernard Ritchie (CAFI)
Bhogilal Leherchand & Pratap Bhogilal (Shree Ram Mills, Bombay)
Chimanlal Damodar Das Seth (Ramesh Silk Mills, Surat)
D.N. Dewan (Madura Mills, Ambasamudram)
D.P. Maloo (Shree Ram Silks, Rishra)
Dinoo Dossabhoy (Laxmi Vishnu Cotton Mills, Solapur)
Girvar Singh & B.N. Singh (Shree Laxmi Synfabs, Dewas)
M.S. Khadbadi (Swastik Dyeing, Bombay)
Martin B.S. Henry (Madura Mills, Ambasamudram)
Narayan Das Shrikishan (Textile Broker, Bombay)

Nigel Kirby (Madura Mills, Ambasamudram)
Niranjan Hiranandani & Surendra Hiranandani (Textile Weaving, Bombay)
O.P. Dhawan (SRTEPC, Bombay)
Pramod Seth & Naveen Kamdar (Dilkhush Dyeing, Bombay)
Raj Nath Singh, Vilas Nath Singh & Viraj Nath Singh (Ahmed Woollen Mills, Thana)
Raja bhau Deshmukh (Ellichpur Cotton Mills near Nagpur)
Ram Gopal Neema (Textile Dealer, Indore)
Ramesh Gangwal (Padma Textiles, Dhulia)
Ranjan Maloo & Sunil Maloo (Shubham Textiles, Dewas)
Ranjit Shahani (CAFI)
Rashesh Mafatlal & Pradeep Mafatlal (Standard Mills, Dewas)
Roger Mora (Michelin, Clermont-Ferrand)
Subodh Sapra (CAFI)

MARKETING:

Bobby Sista (Sista's Advertising)
Harindra Singh & Shailendra Singh (Percept Advertising)
MGM Studios (James Bond Tie-up)
Nishikant Shirodkar (Logo design)

Rupa Sangle (Sista's Advertising)
S.S. Gill (Doordarshan)
Sheila Sista (Sista's Advertising)
Shobha Doctor (Chitrahaar)

SHANTI CHOPRA, SANGEETA CHOPRA & ALL OUR FASHION SHOW MODELS:

Alison Woodham
Anand Balraj
Anna Bredmeyer
Arpana Sharma
Arti Gupta (Surendranath)
Benjamin Gilani
Chabbi Dhariwal
Dalip Tahil

Deepak Parashar
Desiree Gaurishankar
Erica Dsouza
Gazala Chinwala
Javed Khan
Juhi Chawla
Kalpana Iyer
Kimmy Katkar

Kiran Dholakia
Kiran Vairale
Lascelles
Madhu Sapre
Mahesh Anand
Marc Robinson
Mazhar Khan
Mehr Jesia

Michael Vasanth
Namrata Shirodkar
Nandini Sen
Ranjeev Mulchandani
Rubaina Mumtaz
Salim Fatehi
Sangeeta Bijlani
Sharmila Roy Chowdhary

Shobha Rajadhyaksha (De)
Svetlana Casper
Tina Razdan
Ursula Mehta
Vanessa Vaz
Veena Prakash
Zaffar Lalljee

AMEEN SAYANI & ALL THE GUESTS OF S.KUMAR KA FILMI MUKKADAMA:

A.K. Hangal
Aamir Khan
Agha Jani Kashmiri
Ajit

Akhtar Ul Iman
Ali Sardar Jaafri
Amit Khanna
Amit Kumar

Amita
Amitabh Bachchan
Amjad Khan
Amol Palekar

Amrish Puri
Anand Bakshi
Anand Milind
Anil Biswas

Anil Dhawan
Anil Ganguli
Anil Kapoor
Anil Sharma

Anita Guha
Anita Raj
Anjaan
Anu Malik

Anup Jalota	Deepak Tijori	Jaya Bhaduri	Mala Sinha	P. Jairaj	Ram Mohan
Anupam Kher	Deepti Naval	Jaymala (Adarsh)	Manhar Udhas	Padma Khanna	Ramanand Sagar
Anuradha Paudwal	Dheeraj	Joginder	Manmohan Krishna	Padmini Kapila	Ramesh & Seema Deo
Anwar Husain	Dhumal	Johnny Lever	Manna Dey	Padmini Kolhapure	Ramesh Sharma
Arabind Sen	Dina Pathak	Johnny Whisky	Manorama	Paintal	Ramesh Talwar
Aruna Irani	Dinesh Hingoo	Joy Mukherji	Maruti	Pandit Girish	Rameshwari
Asad Bhopali	Dinesh Thakur	Jr. Mehmood	Master Bittu	Pankaj Udhas	Randhir Kapoor
Asha Chandra	Dr. Shriram Lagoo	Jyoti Swaroop	Master Raju	Parikshat Sahni	Ranjeet
Asha Parekh	Dulari	K.B. Pathak	Maya Govind	Parveen Kaul	Ravi
Asha Sachdev	Faiz Ahmed Faiz	K.K. Shukla	Mayur	Peenaz Masani	Ravi Tandon
Ashok Roy	Farida Jalal	Kader Khan	Meenakshi Sheshadri	Phani Majumdar	Ravindra Jain
Asit Sen	Farooq Shaikh	Kaifi Azmi	Mehboob Khan	Poonam Dhillon	Raza Murad
Asrani	G.M. Durrani	Kajal Kiran	Mehdi Hassan	Pradeep Kumar	Rehana Sultan
Aziz Nazan	G.R. Kamat	Kalpana Iyer	Mehmood	Prakash Mehra	Rita Bhaduri
Aziz Qaisi	Gauhar Kanpuri	Kalyanji Anandji	Meraj	Pran	Rohini Hattangadi
B.K. Adarsh	Gayatri	Kamini Kaushal	Minoo Brothers	Pratima Devi	Romesh Sharma
B.M. Vyas	Ghulam Ali	Kamleshwar	Mirza Brothers	Prayag Raj	Roopesh Kumar
B.R. Chopra	Gopi Krishan	Kanan Kaushal	Mirza Musharraf	Preeti Sagar	Runa Laila
B.R. Ishara	Govind Moonis	Kanchan Mattu	Mohan Choti	Prem Anand Moti Sagar	S.H. Bihari
Babban Khan	Gulshan Bawra	Kanu Roy	Mohan Sehgal	Prem Chopra	S.M. Abbas
Bappi Lahiri	Gulshan Grover	Kanwaljeet	Mohd. Rafi	Prem Dhawan	S.M. Sagar
Basu Bhattacharya	Gulzar	Kaushal Bharti	Monty	Prema Narayan	S.M. Yusuf
Basu Chatterji	Harindranath Chattopadhyaya	Kavita Krishnamurti	Mrs. Mehboob Khan	Premnath	S.N. Tripathi
Bhanu Athaiyya	Harmesh Malhotra	Kedar Sharma	Mubarak Begum	Priyadarshini	Sachin
Bharat Kapoor	Hasan Kamal	Khaiyyam	Mukesh Khanna	Pt Narendra Sharma	Sadhana Singh
Bharat Vyas	Hasrat Jaipuri	Kiran Kumar	Mukri	Qamar Jalalabadi	Saeed Jaffrey
Bhimsain	Hemlata	Kiran Vairale	Murad	R. Jhalani	Saeed Rahi
Bhupendra	Hina Kausar	Kishore Kumar	Muzaffar Ali	R.D. Mathur	Sagar Sarhadi
Bindiya Goswami	I.S. Johar	Kishore Sahu	Naaz	Raaj Kumar	Sahir Ludhianvi
Bindu	Iftekhar	Komal Mahuakar	Nabendu Ghosh	Radha Saluja	Sai Paranjape
Birbal	Imtiaz Khan	Krishan Dhawan	Nadira	Raghunath Seth	Salim
Brahmachari	Indiraji	Kulwant Jani	Nana Palsikar	Rahul Rawail	Sardar Malik
C. Arjun	Indivar	Lata Mangeshkar	Nanda	Raj Babbar	Sarika
C. Ramchandra	Indrani Mukherjee	Laxmi Chhaya	Naqsh Lyallpuri	Raj Khosla	Saroj Khan
C.S. Dubey	Iqbal Qureshi	Leela Mishra	Narendra Chanchal	Raj Kishore	Satish Bhatnagar
Chand Usmani	Ismat Chughtai	Lekh Tandon	Narendra Nath	Rajan Haskar	Satyajit
Chandra Barot	Jagdeep	M. Rajan	Naresh Saigal	Rajendra Bhatia	Satyen Kappu
Chandrashekhar	Jagdish Raj	M.G. Hashmat	Naseeruddin Shah	Rajendra Kumar	Shabana Azmi
Charandas Shokh	Jagjit & Chitra Singh	Mac Mohan	Naushad	Rajendra Nath	Shabbir Kumar
Chunky Pandey	Jaidev	Madan Joshi	Navin Nischol	Rajinder Krishen	Shafi Inamdar
Daisy Irani	Jaishree T	Madan Puri	Nazir Husain	Rajinder S Bedi, Faiz,	Shah Rukh Khan
Danny Denzongpa	Jalal Agha	Madhu Malini	Neelam Mehra	Rehman, Jennifer	Shahid Bijnori
Dara Singh	Jani Babu	Mahendra Kapoor	Nirupa Roy	Rajkumari	Shailendra Singh
David	Janki Daas	Mahendra Sandhu	Nitin Mukesh	Rakesh Bedi	Shailey Shailendra
Deb Mukherji	Javed	Mahipal	Om Prakash	Rakesh Pandey	Shakila Bano Bhopali
Deepak Parashar	Javed Jaffrey	Majrooh	Om Shivpuri	Rakesh Roshan	Shakti Kapoor

Shakti Samanta	Shyama	Sunil Dutt	Talat Aziz	Varma Malik	Vithal bhai Patel
Sharda	Sitara Devi	Sunil Gavaskar	Talat Mehmood	Veena	Waheeda Rehman
Shashi Kapoor	Sonia Sahni	Supriya Pathak	Tamanna	Vijay Arora	Yunus Parvez
Shashikala	Sonik Omi	Suraj Sanim	Tanuja	Vijay Bhatt	Zahida
Shatrughan Sinha	Subhash Gai	Surendra Kaur	Tariq	Vijay Sadana	Zarina Wahaab
Shetty	Sudesh Kumar	Surendra Nath	Trilok Kapoor	Viju Khote	Zia Sarhadi
Shivraj	Sudha Chopra	Suresh Wadkar	Tun Tun (Uma Devi)	Vikram	
Shobha Khote	Sudhir (Bhagwan)	Sushma Shreshtha	Urmila Bhatt	Vinod Mehra	
Shoma Anand	Sujeet Kumar	Tabassum	Usha Khanna & Sawan Kumar	Vinod Sharma	

OUR BRAND AMBASSADORS & OTHER CELEBRITIES:

Amitabh Bachchan	Kapil Dev	Nitin Mongia	Shahrukh Khan	Sushmita Sen
Dicky Rutnagar	M.F. Husain	Pierce Brosnan	Sourav Ganguly	Zakir Hussain
Hrithik Roshan	Mohinder Amarnath	Sachin Tendulkar	Steve Waugh	

PERSONAL

Balchand Jain	Dr. Mohanlal B. Popat	Pratap Ozha	Dr. Rajeev Sharma	Sarla ben Mistry	Vimalchand Jhanjari
Bhaskar Ganu	Narsinghdas Gupta	Premchand Bakliwal	Dr. S.N. Subbarao	Shantikumar Kapadia	

TEAM

A. Narendra Chettlyar	Ashok Shah	Dharmendra Kumar Singh	Jamunadas Jasnani	Mansukh Patel	Pradeep Sthapak
A.B. Pandya	Ashok Singh	Dhirendra P. Shroff	Janardan Salvi	Mukesh Bachhuka	Praveen Kumar Patankar
A.K. Goyle	Ashwin Trivedi	Dilip Bahura	Jeevan Singh Tawar	Mukesh Fadia	Praveen Shah
A.K. Shandilya	Avinash Madavi	Dilip Barot	Jitendra Chowdhary	Murlidhar, Shrigopal, Govind Inani	Prem B. Vaid
A.K. Upadhyay	B.K. Bharadwaj	Dilip Choubey	Jyotikumar Jhunjhunwala	N. Ram	Prem Prakash Chaurasia
A.M. Raut	Babulal C. Shah	Dilip Karmakar	K. Sayi Krishnan	N. Srinivasan	Prem Prakash Kamal
Dr. A.S. Ghag	Bairam Vakil	G. Reghunatha Kurup	K.K. Maini	N.L. Longani	Pukh Raj Bhandi
Aatam Prakash &	Balchandra Patel	G.D. Bansal	Kamlakar Modak	N.R. Raut	Punamchand Daga
Surendra Kumar Arora	Baliram & Girdharilal Hasanand	G.D. Wadekar	Kamlesh Nirwani	Narayan Verma	R. Krishna
Aloka Banerjee	Bankatlal Bang	G.P. Singh	Kanhaiyalal Abhani	Narottamlal & Rajeev Berry	R.K. Poojari
Amar Singh Rathore	Bhagawat Ingle	Gilbert D'costa	Karamshi bhai Patel	Nathmal Rampuria	R.K. Shah
Amarnath Aggarwal	Bhagirat Mal Indoriya	Girish P Daryani	Kishore Dutta	Nihalchand Bakliwal	R.N. Bhaskar
Ambika Nair	Bharat Vindara	Golaram Atlani	Lalit Bhatt	Nilesh Salvi	R.N. Joshi
Amitabh Tiwari	Bhartan Ghia	Brig. H.B.S. Grewal	Laxmidas Kamat	O.P. Pacheria	R.P. Bora
Anil Gour	Brijesh Narayan Singh	H.P. Gupta	Lokendra Bakliwal	Om Prakash Trivedi	R.P. Shah
Anil Kumar Gupta	Chandrakant Mehta	Haresh H. Daryani	Lokendra Jain	P.M. Vyas	R.S. Ahuja
Anil Sharma	Chimanlal Kapasi	Harish Khurana	M.S. Hardikar	P.V. Rajan	R.S. Kharkar
Arjun Duduskar	D.C. Bilimoria	Harshad Shah	Madanlal Maloo	Pankaj Mhatre	R.V. Naik
Asha Vadhya	Col. D.K. Ghosh	Hasmukh Shah	Mahendra Singh Parihar	Pankaj Shah	R.V. Pai
Ashok Arora	D.R. Pendse	Hemchandra Maheshwari	Mahesh Ayare	Pannalal & Abhay Dave	Rajatkumar Nag
Ashok Kumar Neema	Dattatray Raykar	Ishwarsingh Metwadia	Manmohan Mehta	Parvez Damania	Rajendra Kadam
Ashok Kumar Tiwari	Devraj & Prakash Ranka	J.S. Saini	Manoj Dhiman	Pradeep Chavan	Rajendra Mehta

Rajesh Karmarkar	Rekha Jagdale	S.P. Banerjee	Shaktivardhan Nigam	Sudhir bhai Shah	Tushar Rawal
Rajesh Pipada	Rishikesh Mishra	S.P. Singh	Shashikant Sharma	Sudhir Bhawate	V.K. Jain
Rakesh & Mukesh Neema	S. Muthu	Sachin Shrivastav	Shiv Sharma	Sudhir More	V.R. Joshi
Ram Vilas Yadav	S.C. Dalal	Salim Khan	Shyam Bihari Khanna	Sudhir Tiwari	V.R. Shanbagh
Ramalaxmi Tataparti	Wg. Cdr. S.D. Sinha	Sampatlal Minni	Shyam Malpani	Sujata Dutta	Vaidehi Randive
Ramesh Doshi	S.K. Bhoan	Sandeep Jambheker	Shyamala Ananthraman	Sukhmal Jain	Vijay Kalantri
Ramesh Jain	S.K. Biyani	Sangeeta Rane	Shyamdhar Mishra	Sunil Kumar Pathak	Vilas Gharat
Ramesh Laddha	S.K. Luharuka	Sanjay Chhabra	Sohan Patel	Sunil Kumar Sharma	Vipin Kumar Matkar
Ramesh Singhal	S.K. Mundra	Sanjay Vadhavana	Somnath Singh Kharwar	Susan Shinde	Virendra Bhatt
Ranjan Maloo	Col. S.K. Raje	Santosh Patel	Subhash Kataria	Tilak Raj, Sudesh &	Viroo Rangnekar
Rati bhai Jain	S.K. Thakral	Sawan Soni	Sudesh Vyas	Sumati Arora	Vitthalkumar Bangera
Ravi Sharma	S.M. Borkar	Shailendra Verma	Sudhakar Nemavarkar	Tulsi Ram Vishwakarma	William Fernandes

A FEW MORE...

Aasha Sisoudiya	Devkaran Solanki	Krishna Damthe	Rajani Pawar	Rekha Verma	Suman Solanki
Anita Raghuwanshi	Dharmendra Ghoraval	Krishnakant Mandloi	Rajendra Patel	Satyanarayan Kumawat	Sunil Patel
Anita Rathore	Geeta Bai Verma	Lalita Bai Kadam	Raju Verma	Shanta Bai	Sunil R. Patel
Ankesh Malviya	Geeta Jhala	Late Gagaram Badad	Rakesh Yadav	Shiv Narayan Yadav	Sunita Joshi
Antar Singh	Gokul Patel	Laxman Singh Dodiya	Rambagas Patel	Shrinath Mishra	Sunita Rajoriya
Avinash Thakur	Jagdev Dubey	Mahesh Patel	Rameshwar Verma	Shyamdeo Yadav	Susheela Parihar
Bhagwanta Bai	Jagdish Patel	Makhan Patel	Ramgopal Patel	Siddharth Bendkhale	Uma Nihare
Bhupesh Bhati	Jagnnath Kushwah	Mithlesh Yadav	Ramsingh Chouhan	Soram Bai	Vijay Choudhary
Brijesh Choudhary	Jarnail Singh	Nalini Charde	Ramu Bai Dugal	Srawan Bairagi	Vikram Patel
Chander	Jitendra Pathak	Nirmala Verma	Ranjana Khadse	Subhash Patel	Vinod Kumar Singh
Dariyav Singh	Kailash Giri Goswami	Radha Jaiswal	Ranjeet Singh	Subhash S. Patel	
Dattaram Sutar	Kishor Kasare	Rahul Sharma	Ravindra Yadav	Subhash Yadav	

A big salute to our entire team, trade and dealer network that spans the length and breadth of the country. Also, the countless others who we may not have named. Thank you for giving your best. We are utterly grateful to you all.

- SHAMBHU KUMAR

SPECIAL THANKS

Shambhu Kumar Kasliwal	Leena Kasliwal	Anuradha Kasliwal	Mukul Kasliwal	Girija Goenka	Sneha Kirloskar
Rajkumari Kasliwal	Pratibha Kasliwal	Manoj Kasliwal	Neerja Birla	Dhvani Kaul	Utkarsh Kasliwal
Sumati Kumar Kasliwal	Vikas Kasliwal	Nitin Kasliwal	Pratik Desai	Gaurav Kaul	Dhruv Kasliwal

& the rest of the entire family for all their love, support & blessings

Ashok Kumar Goyle	Lalit Bhatt	Narsinghdas Gupta	Punamchand Daga	Rupa Sangle	Subhash Kataria
Ashok Shah	Lokendra Jain	Om Prakash Pacheria	Rajeev Berry	Shanti Chopra &	Surendra Kumar Modi
Bobby Sista	Madhushree Modak-Ghatge	Panna Zaveri	Rajendra Kumar Mehta	Sangeeta Chopra	Vaman Apte
Gopal Inani	Mukesh Fadia	Pannalal Dave	Rajkumar Jhanjari	Shubh Karan Luharuka	
Kamal Kishore Maini	Nareshchand Sethi	Prakash Ranka	Ramesh Laddha	Shyam Sunder Kejriwal	

for taking out their valuable time to give interviews

Clare Misquitta	G. Reghunatha Kurup	K.R. Mahadevan (Mohan)	Manoj Jain	Rajil Sayani	Shubhra Krishan
Deepak Jetha & Vishal Jain	Jitendra Chowdhary	Kshiti Nijhawan Agrawal	Priya Venkataraman	Ravendra Singh Bhadauria	Tejaswini Apte-Rahm

for all the inputs & back-end work

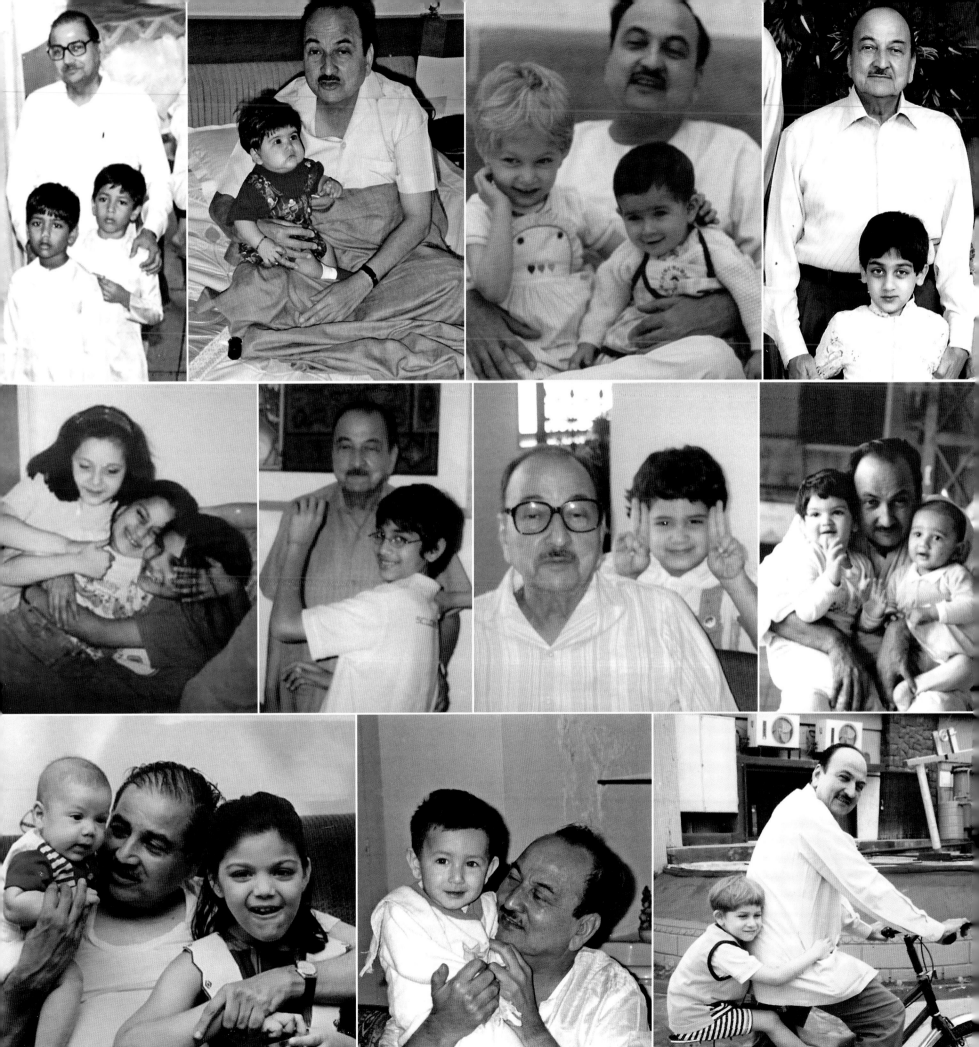

ABOUT THE AUTHOR

Image Courtesy: Brunch

Best known for her long association with Femina, which she edited for 12 years, Sathya Saran is also the author of a diverse variety of books that include fiction and biographies. Currently Consulting Editor with Penguin Random House, Sathya also teaches fashion journalism at NIFT Mumbai, Kangra and Srinagar.